Courtesy J. B. Lippincott Co.

NEWSTEAD ABBEY, BYRON'S ANCESTRAL HOME
(See Vol. I for article on Newstead)

Courtesy J. B. Lippincott Co.

STOKE POGIS, THE SCENE OF GRAY'S "ELEGY"

Courtesy, Great Western Railway of England

OXFORD

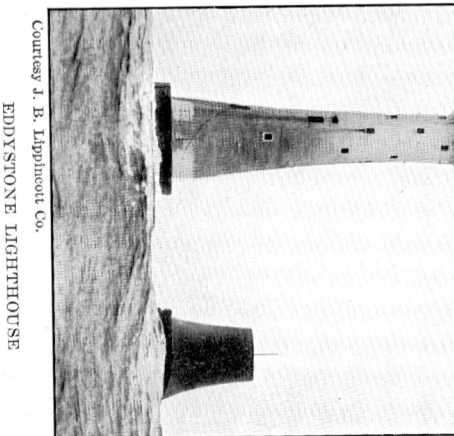

Courtesy J. B. Lippincott Co.
EDDYSTONE LIGHTHOUSE
The stump is part of Smeaton's earlier lighthouse

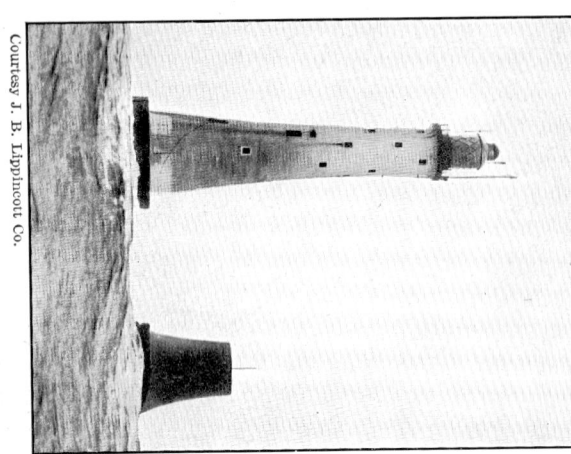

ST. MARTIN'S CHURCH, CANTERBURY
(See Vol. I for article on Canterbury)

EDINBURGH CASTLE AND NATIONAL GALLERY

OLD GREYFRIAR'S CHURCH, EDINBURGH

HOLYROOD PALACE, EDINBURGH

IV

ENGLISH LITERARY SHRINES
(*Continued*)

STOKE POGIS*

BY CHARLES T. CONGDON

It was a comfort as I came out of the Albert Memorial Chapel, and rejoined nature upon the Terrace, to mutter to myself those fine lines which not a hundred years ago everybody knew by heart: "The boast of heraldry, the pomp of power, And all that beauty, all that wealth ere gave, Await alike th' inevitable hour. The paths of glory lead but to the grave,"—a verse which I found it not bad to remember as in the Chapel Royal I gazed upon the helmets, and banners, and insignia of many a defunct Knight of the Garter. I wondered if posterity would care much for George the Fourth, or Third, or Second, or First, whose portraits I had just been gazing at; I was sure that a good many would remember the recluse scholar of Pembroke Hall, the Cambridge Professor of Modern History, who cared for nothing but ancient history; who projected twenty

*From "Reminiscenses of a Journalist." By special arrangement with, and by permission of, the publishers, Houghton, Mifflin Copyright, 1884. Mr. Congdon was, for many years, under Horace Greeley, a leading editorial writer for the New York "Tribune."

great poems, and finished only one or two; who spent his life in commenting upon Plato and studying botany, and in writing letters to his friend Mason; and who with a real touch of Pindar in his nature, was content to fiddle-faddle away his life. He died at last of a most unpoetical gout in the stomach, leaving behind him a cartload of memoranda, and fifty fragments of fine things; and yet I, a stranger from a far distant shore, was about to make a little pilgrimage to his tomb, and all for the sake of that "Elegy Written in a Country Churchyard," which has so held its own while a hundred bulkier things have been forgotten.

The church itself is an interesting but not remarkable edifice, old, small, and solidly built in a style common enough in England. Nothing, however, could be more in keeping with the associations of the scene. The very humility of the edifice has a property of its own, for anything more magnificent would jar upon the feelings, as the monument in the Park does most decidedly. It was Gray's wish that he might be buried here, near the mother whom he loved so well; otherwise he could hardly have escaped the posthumous misfortune of a tomb in Westminster Abbey or St. Paul's. In such case the world would have missed one of the most charming of associations, and the great poem the most poetical of its features. For surely it was fit that he who sang so touchingly of the dead here sleeping, should find near them his last resting-place; that when the pleasant toil in libraries was over, the last folio closed by those industrious hands, the last manuscript collated, and the last flower picked for the herbarium, he who here so tenderly sang of the emptiness of earthly honors and the nothingness of wordly success should be buried humbly near those whom he best loved, and where all the moral of his teaching might be perpetually illustrated. I wondered, as I stood there, whether Horace Walpole ever thought it worth his while, for the sake of that early friendship which was so rudely broken, to come there, away from the haunts of fashion, or from his plaything villa at Strawberry Hill, to muse for a moment over the grave of one who rated pedigrees and peerages at their just value. Probably my Lord Orford was never guilty of such a piece of sentimentality. He was thinking too much of his pictures and coins and eternal bric-a-brac for that.

A stone set in the outside of the church indicates the spot near which the poet is buried. I was very anxious to see the interior of the edifice, and, fortunately I found the sexton busy in the neighborhood. There was nothing, however, remarkable to be seen, after sixpence had opened the door, except perhaps the very largest pew which these eyes ever beheld. It belonged to the Penn family, descendants of drab-coated and sweet-voiced William Penn, whose seat is in the neighborhood. I do not know what that primitive Quaker would have said to such an enormous reservation of space in the house of God for the sole use and behoof of two or three aristocratic worshipers. Probably few of my readers have ever seen such a pew as that. It was not so much a pew as a room. It was literally walled off, and quite set apart from the plebeian portion of the sanctuary, was carpeted, and finished with comfortable arm-chairs, and in the middle of it was a stove. The occupants could look out and over at the altar, but the rustics could not look in and at them. The Squire might have smoked or read novels, or my lady might have worked worsted or petted her poodle through the service, without much scandal. The pew monopolized so much room that there was little left for the remainder of the "miserable offenders," but I suspect that there was quite enough for all who came to pray. For it was, as I have said, literally a country church; and those who sleep near it were peasants.

It is difficult to comprehend the whole physiognomy of the poem, if I may use the expression, without seeing the spot which it commemorates. I take it for granted that the reader is familiar with it. There are "those rugged elms," and there is "that yew tree's shade." There are "the frail memorials," "with uncouth rhymes and shapeless sculpture decked;" there "the name, the years, spelt by the unlettered muse;" and the holy texts strewn round "that teach the rustic moralist to die." There is still "the ivy-mantled tower," tho the "moping owl" that evening did not "to the moon complain," partly because there was no moon to complain to, and possibly because there was no moping owl in the tower. But there was one little circumstance which I may be pardoned for mentioning. Gray, somehow, has the reputation of being an artificial

ENGLISH LITERARY SHRINES

poet, yet for one who wrote so little poetry he makes a good many allusions to childhood and children. As I passed through the Park on my way to the churchyard, I encountered a group of merry boys and girls playing about the base of the monument; and I recalled that verse which Gray wrote for the Elegy, and afterward discarded, under the impression that it made the parenthesis too long.

> There scatter'd oft, the earliest of the year,
>   By hands unseen are showers of violets found;
> The redbreast loves to build and warble there,
>   And little footsteps lightly print the ground.

I have often wondered how Gray could bear to give up these sweet, tender and most natural lines. I have sometimes surmised that he thought them a little too much like Ambrose Philips's verses about children—Namby Pamby Philips, as the Pope set nicknamed that unfortunate writer.

I lingered about the churchyard until that long twilight, of which we know nothing in America, began to grow dimmer and dimmer. If it was still before, it seemed all the stiller now. I was glad that I had waited so long, because by doing so I understood all the better how true the Elegy is to nature. The neighborhood, with its agreeable variety of meadow and wood, has all the hundred charms of the gentle and winning English scenery. The hush, hardly broken even by the songs of the birds, brought forcibly to my mind that beautiful line of the Elegy: "And all the air a solemn stillness holds;" while that other line: "Now fades the glimmering landscape on the sight," is exactly true. The landscape did glimmer, and as I watched the sun go down, I pleased myself with the fancy that I was sitting just where the poet sat, as he revolved those lines which the world has got by heart. Just then came the cry of the cattle, and I knew why Gray wrote: "The lowing herd winds slowly o'er the lea," nor did I fail to encounter a plowman homeward plodding his weary way.

As I strolled listlessly back to the station, there was such a serenity on the earth about me, and in the sky above me, that I could easily give myself to gentle memories and poetic dreams. I recalled the spring-time of life, when I learned this famous Elegy by heart as a pleasant task, and, as yet unsophisticated by critical notions, accepted it as perfect. I thought of innummerable things which I had read about it; of the long and patient revision which its author gave it, year after year, keeping it in his desk, and then sending it, a mere pamphlet, with no flourish of trumpets, into the world. Many an ancient figure came to lend animation to the scene. Horace Walpole in his lace coat and spruce wig went mincing by; the mother of Gray, with her sister, measured lace for the customers who came to her little shop in London; the wags of Pembroke College, graceless varlets, raise an alarm of fire that they may see the frightened poet drop from the window, half dead with alarm; old Foulis, the Glasgow printer, volunteers to send from his press such a luxurious edition of Gray's poems as the London printers can not match; Dr. Johnson, holding the page to his eyes, growls over this stanza, and half-grudgingly praises that. I had spent perhaps the pleasantest day which the fates vouchsafed me during my sojourn in England; and here I was back again in Slough Station, ready to return to the noisy haunts of men. The train came rattling up, and the day with Gray was over.

HAWORTH*

BY THEODORE F. WOLFE

Other Brontë shrines have engaged us,—Guiseley, where Patrick Brontë was married and Neilson worked as a mill-girl; the lowly Thornton home, where Charlotte was born; the cottage where she visited Harriet Martineau; the school where she found Caroline Helstone and Rose and Jessy Yorke; the Fieldhead, Lowood, and Thornfield of her tales; the Villette where she knew her hero; but it is the bleak Haworth hilltop where the Brontës wrote the wonderful books and lived the pathetic lives that most attracts and longest holds our steps. Our way is along Airedale, now a highway of toil and trade, desolated by the need of hungry poverty and greed of hungrier wealth; meads are replaced by blocks of grimy huts, groves are supplanted by factory chimneys that assoil earth and

*From "A Literary Pilgrimage." By arrangement with, and by permission of, the publishers, J. B. Lippincott Co. Copyright, 1895.

heaven, the one "shining" stream is filthy with the refuse of many mills.

At Keighley our walk begins, and altho we have no peas in our "Pilgrim shoon," the way is heavy with memories of the sad sisters Brontë who so often trod the dreary miles which bring us to Haworth. The village street, steep as a roof, has a pavement of rude stones, upon which the wooden shoes of the villagers clank with an unfamiliar sound. The dingy houses of gray stone, barren and ugly in architecture, are huddled along the incline and encroach upon the narrow street. The place and its situation are a proverb of ugliness in all the countryside; one dweller in Airedale told us that late in the evening of the last day of creation it was found that a little rubbish was left, and out of that Haworth was made. But, grim and rough as it is, the genius of a little woman has made the place illustrious and draws to it visitors from every quarter of the world. We are come in the "glory season" of the moors, and as we climb through the village we behold above and beyond it vast undulating sweeps of amethyst-tinted hills rising circle beyond circle,—all now one great expanse of purple bloom stirred by zephyrs which waft to us the perfume of the heather.

At the hill-top we come to the Black Bull Inn, where one Brontë drowned his genius in drink, and from our apartment here we look upon all the shrines we seek. The inn stands at the church-yard gates, and is one of the landmarks of the place. Long ago preacher Grimshaw flogged the loungers from its taproom into chapel; here Wesley and Whitefield lodged when holding meetings on the hill-top; here Brontë's predecessor took refuge from his riotous parishioners, finally escaping through the low casement at the back,—out of which poor Branwell Brontë used to vault when his sisters asked for him at the door. This inn is a quaint structure, low-eaved and cosy; its furniture is dark with age. We sleep in a bed once occupied by Henry J. Raymond,* and so lofty that steps are provided to ascend its heights. Our meals are served in the old-fashioned parlor to which Branwell came. In a nook between the fireplace and the before-mentioned casement stood the tall arm-chair, with square seat and quaintly carved back, which was reserved for him.

The landlady denied that he was summoned to entertain travelers here; "he never needed to be sent for, he came fast enough of himself." His wit and conviviality were usually the life of the circle, but at times he was mute and abstracted and for hours together "would just sit and sit in his corner there." She described him as a "little, red-haired, light-complexioned chap, cleverer than all his sisters put together. What they put in their books they got from him," quoth she, reminding us of the statement in Grundy's Reminiscences that Branwell declared he invented the plot and wrote the major part of "Wuthering Heights." Certain it is he possest transcending genius and that in

*In the editorial sense, the founder of the New York "Times." Mr. Raymond died in 1869, eighteen years after the paper was started.

this room that genius was slain. Here he received the message of renunciation from his depraved mistress which finally wrecked his life; the landlady, entering after the messenger had gone, found him in a fit on the floor. Emily Brontë's rescue of her dog, an incident recorded in "Shirley," occurred at the inn door.

The graveyard is so thickly sown with blackened tombstones that there is scant space for blade or foliage to relieve its dreariness, and the villagers, for whom the yard is a thoroughfare, step from tomb to tomb; in the time of the Brontës the village women dried their linen on these graves. Close to the wall which divides the church-yard from the vicarage is a plain stone set by Charlotte Brontë to mark the grave of Tabby, the faithful servant who served the Brontës from their childhood till all but Charlotte were dead. The very ancient church-tower still "rises dark from the stony enclosure of its yard;" the church itself has been remodeled and much of its romantic interest destroyed. No interments have been made in the vaults beneath the aisles since Mr. Brontë was laid there. The site of the Brontë pew is by the chancel; here Emily sat in the farther corner, Anne next and Charlotte by the door, within a foot of the spot where her ashes now lie.

A former sacristan remembered to have seen Thackeray and Miss Martineau sitting with Charlotte in the pew. And here, almost directly above her sepulcher, she stood one summer morning and gave herself in marriage to the man who served for her as "faithfully and long as did Jacob for Rachel." The Brontë tablet in

ENGLISH LITERARY SHRINES

the wall bears a uniquely pathetic record, its twelve lines registering eight deaths, of which Mr. Brontë's at the age of eighty-five, is the last. On a side aisle is a beautiful stained window inscribed "To the Glory of God, in Memory of Charlotte Brontë, by an American citizen." The list shows that most of the visitors come from America, and it was left for a dweller in that far land to set up here almost the only voluntary memento of England's great novelist. A worn page of the register displays the tremulous autograph of Charlotte as she signs her maiden name for the last time, and the signatures of the witnesses to her marriage, —Miss Wooler, of "Roe Head," Ellen Nussy, who is the E of Charlotte's letters and the Caroline of "Shirley."

The vicarage and its garden are out of a corner of the church-yard and separated from it by a low wall. A lane lies along one side of the church-yard and leads from the street to the vicarage gates. The garden, which was Emily's care, where she tended stunted shrubs and borders of unresponsive flowers and where Charlotte planted the currant-bushes, is beautiful with foliage and flowers, and its boundary wall is overtopped by a screen of trees which shuts out the depressing prospect of the graves from the vicarage windows and makes the place seem less "a church-yard home" than when the Brontës inhabited it. The dwelling is of gray stone, two stories high, of plain and somber aspect. A wing is added, the little window-panes are replaced by larger squares, the stone floors are removed or concealed, curtains—for-

SEEING EUROPE WITH FAMOUS AUTHORS

bidden by Mr. Brontë's dread of fire—shade the window, and the once bare interior is furbished and furnished in modern style; but the arrangement of the apartments is unchanged.

Most interesting of these is the Brontë parlor, at the left of the entrance; here the three curates of "Shirley" used to take tea with Mr. Brontë and were upbraided by Charlotte for their intolerance; here the sisters discust their plots and read each other's MSS.; here they transmuted the sorrows of their lives into the stories which make the name of Brontë immortal; here Emily, "her imagination occupied with Wuthering Heights," watched in the darkness to admit Branwell coming late and drunken from the Black Bull; here Charlotte, the survivor of all, paced the night-watches in solitary anguish, haunted by the vanished faces, the voices forever stilled, the echoing footsteps that came no more. Here, too, she lay in her coffin. The room behind the parlor was fitted by Charlotte for Nichols's study. On the right was Brontë's study, and behind it the kitchen, where the sisters read with their books propt on the table before them while they worked, and where Emily (prototype of "Shirley"), bitten by a dog at the gate of the lane, took one of Tabby's glowing irons from the fire and cauterized the wound, telling no one till danger was past.

Above the parlor is the chamber in which Charlotte and Emily died, the scene of Nichols's loving ministrations to his suffering wife. Above Brontë's study was his chamber; the adjoining children's study was later Branwell's apartment and the theater of the most terrible

ENGLISH LITERARY SHRINES

tragedies of the stricken family; here that ill-fated youth writhed in the horrors of mania-a-potu; here Emily rescued him—stricken with drunken stupor—from his burning couch, as "Jane Eyre" saved Rochester; here he breathed out his blighted life erect upon his feet, his pockets filled with love-letters from the perfidious woman who brought his ruin. Even now the isolated site of the parsonage, its environment of graves and wild-moors, its exposure to the fierce winds of the long winters, make it unspeakably dreary; in the Brontës' time it must have been cheerless indeed. Its influence darkened the lives of the inmates and left its fateful impression upon the books here produced. Visitors are rarely admitted to the vicarage; among those against whom its doors have been closed is the gifted daughter of Charlotte's literary idol, to whom "Jane Eyre" was dedicated, Thackeray.

By the vicarage lane were the cottage of Tabby's sister, the school the Brontës daily visited, and the sexton's dwelling where the curates lodged. Behind the vicarage a savage expanse of gorse and heather rises to the horizon and stretches many miles away; a path oft-trodden by the Brontës leads between low walls from their home to this open moor, their habitual resort in childhood and womanhood. The higher plateaus afford a wide prospect, but, despite the August bloom and fragrance and the delightful play of light and shadow along the sinuous sweeps, the aspect of the bleak, treeless, houseless waste of uplands is even now dispiriting; when frosts have destroyed its verdure, and wintry skies frown above, its gloom and desolation must be terrible beyond description. Remembering that the sisters found even these usually dismal moors a welcome relief from their tomb of a dwelling, we may appreciate the utter dreariness of their situation and the pathos of Charlotte's declaration, "I always dislike to leave Haworth, it takes so long to be content again after I return."

GAD'S HILL*

BY THEODORE F. WOLFE

"To go to Gad's Hill," said Dickens, in a note of invitation, "you leave Charing Cross at nine o'clock by North Kent Railway for Higham." Guided by these directions and equipped with a letter from Dickens's son, we find ourselves gliding eastward among the chimneys of London and, a little later, emerging into the fields of Kent,—Jingle's region of "apples, cherries, hops, and women." The Thames is on our left; we pass many river-towns,—Dartford where Wat Tyler lived, Gravesend where Pocahontas died,—but most of our way is through the open country, where we have glimpses of "fields," "parks," and leafy lanes, with here and there picturesque camps of gipsies or of peripatetic rascals "goin' a-hoppin.'" From wretched Higham a walk of half an hour among

*From "A Literary Pilgrimage." By arrangement with, and by permission of, the publishers, J. B. Lippincott Co. Copyright, 1895.

ENGLISH LITERARY SHRINES

orchards and between hedges of wild-rose and honeysuckle brings us to the hill which Shakespeare and Dickens have made classic ground, and soon we see, above the tree tops, the glittering vane which surmounted the home of the world's greatest novelist.

The name Gad's (Vagabond's) Hill is a survival of the time when the depredations of highwaymen upon "pilgrims going to Canterbury with rich offerings and traders riding to London with fat purses" gave to this spot the ill repute it had in Shakespeare's day; it was here he located Falstaff's great exploit. The tuft of evergreens which crowns the hill about Dickens' retreat is the remnant of thick woods once closely bordering the highway, in which the "men in buckram" lay concealed, and the robbery of the Franklin was committed in front of the spot where the Dickens house stands. By this road passed Chaucer, who had property near by, gathering from the pilgrims his "Canterbury Tales." In all time to come the great master of romance who came here to live and die will be worthily associated with Shakespeare and Chaucer in the renown of Gad's Hill.

In becoming possessor of this place Dickens realized a dream of his boyhood and ambition of his life. In one of his travelers' sketches he introduces a "queer small boy" (himself) gazing at Gad's Hill House and predicting his future ownership, which the author finds annoying "because it happens to be my house and I believe what he said was true." When at last the place was for sale, Dickens did not wait to examine it; he never was inside the house until he went to direct its repair. Eighteen hundred pounds was the price; a thousand more were expended for enlargement of the grounds and alterations of the house, which, despite his declaration that he had "stuck bits upon it in all manner of ways," did not greatly change it from what it was when it became the goal of his childish aspirations. At first it was his summer residence merely,—his wife came with him the first summer,—but three years later he sold Tavistock House, and Gad's Hill was thenceforth his home. From the bustle and din of the city he returned to the haunts of his boyhood to find restful quiet and time for leisurely work among these "blessed woods and fields" which had ever held his heart. For nine years after the death of Dickens Gad's Hill was occupied by his oldest son; its ownership has since twice or thrice changed.

Its elevated site and commanding view render it one of the most conspicuous, as it is one of the most lovely, spots in Kent. The mansion is an unpretentious, old-fashioned, two-storied structure of fourteen rooms. Its brick walls are surmounted by Mansard roofs above which rises a bell-turret; a pillared portico, where Dickens sat with his family on summer evenings, shades the front entrance; wide bay-windows project upon either side; flowers and vines clamber upon the walls, and a delightfully home-like air prevades the place. It seems withal a modest seat for one who left half a million dollars at his death. At the right of the entrance-hall we see Dickens's library and study, a cosy room shown in the picture of

ENGLISH LITERARY SHRINES

"The Empty Chair;" here are shelves which held his books; the panels he decorated with counterfeit bookbacks; the nook where perched the mounted remains of his raven, the "Grip" of "Barnaby Rudge." By this bay-window, whence he could look across the lawn to the cedars beyond the highway, stood his chair and the desk where he wrote many of the works by which the world will know him alway. Behind the study was his billiard-room, and upon the opposite side of the hall the parlor, with the dining-room adjoining it at the back, both bedecked with the many mirrors which delighted the master.

Opening out of these rooms is a conservatory, paid for out of "the golden shower from America" and completed but a few days before Dickens' death, holding yet the ferns he tended. The dining-room was the scene of much of that emphatic hospitality which it pleased the novelist to dispense, his exuberant spirits making him the leader in all the jollity and conviviality of the board. Here he compounded for bibulous guests his famous "cider-cup of Gad's Hill," and at the same table he was stricken with death; on a couch beneath yonder window, the one nearest the hall, he died on the anniversary of the railway accident which so frightfully imperiled his life. From this window we look out upon a lawn decked with shrubbery and see across undulating cornfields his beloved Cobham. From the parqueted hall, stairs lead to the modest chambers—that of Dickens being above the drawing-room. He lined the stairway with prints of Hogarth's works, and declared he never came down the stairs without pausing to wonder at the sagacity and skill which had produced these masterful pictures of human life.

The house is invested with roses, and parterres of the red geraniums which the master loved are ranged upon every side. It was some fresh manifestation of his passion for these flowers that elicited from his daughter the averment, "Papa, I think when you are an angel your wings will be made of looking-glasses and your crown of scarlet geraniums." Beneath a rose-tree not far from the window where Dickens died, a bed blooming with blue lobelia holds the tiny grave of "Dick" and the tender memorial of the novelist to that "Best of Birds." The row of gleaming limes which shadow the porch was planted by Dickens's own hands. The pedestal of the sundial upon the lawn is a massive balustrade of the old stone bridge at nearby Rochester, which little David Copperfield crossed "footsore and weary" on his way to his aunt, and from which Pickwick contemplated the castle-ruin, the cathedral, the peaceful Medway. At the left of the mansion are the carriage-house and the school-room of Dickens' sons. In another portion of the grounds are his tennis-court and the bowling-green which he prepared, where he became a skilful and tireless player. The broad meadow beyond the lawn was a later purchase, and the many limes which beautify it were rooted by Dickens. Here numerous cricket-matches were played, and he would watch the players or keep the score "The whole day long."

It was in this meadow that he rehearsed his

readings, and his talking, laughing, weeping, and gesticulating here "all to himself" excited among his neighbors suspicion of his insanity. From the front lawn a tunnel constructed by Dickens passes beneath the highway to "The Wilderness," a thickly-wooded shrubbery, where magnificent cedars uprear their venerable forms and many somber firs, survivors of the forest which erst covered the countryside, cluster upon the hill top. Here Dickens's favorite dog, the "Linda" of his letters, lies buried. Amid the leafy seclusion of this retreat, and upon the very spot where Falstaff was routed by Hal and Poins ("the eleven men in buckram"), Dickens erected the chalet sent to him in pieces by Fechter, the upper room of which—up among the quivering boughs, where "birds and butterflies fly in and out, and green branches shoot in at the windows"— Dickens lined with mirrors and used as his study in summer. Of the work produced at Gad's Hill—"A Tale of Two Cities," "The Uncommercial Traveler," "Our Mutual Friend," "The Mystery of Edwin Drood," and many tales and sketches of "All the Year Round"— much was written in this leaf-environed nook; here the master wrought through the golden hours of his last day of conscious life, here he wrote his last paragraph and at the close of that June day let fall his pen, never to take it up again. From the place of the chalet we behold the view which delighted the heart of Dickens—his desk was so placed that his eyes would rest upon this view whenever he raised them from his work—the fields of waving corn, the green expanse of meadows, the sail-dotted river.

SEEING EUROPE WITH FAMOUS AUTHORS

RYDAL MOUNT*

BY WILLIAM HOWITT

As you advance a mile or more on the road from Ambleside toward Grasmere, a lane overhung with trees turns up to the right, and there, at some few hundred yards from the highway, stands the modest cottage of the poet, elevated on Rydal Mount, so as to look out over the surrounding sea of foliage, and to take in a glorious view. Before it, at some distance across the valley, stretches a high screen of bold and picturesque mountains; behind, it is overtowered by a precipitous hill, called Nab-scar; but to the left, you look down over the broad waters of Windermere, and to the right over the still and more embosomed flood of Grasmere.

Whichever way the poet pleases to advance from his house, it must be into scenery of that beauty of mountain, stream, wood, and lake, which has made Cumberland so famous over all England. He may steal away up backward from his gate and ascend into the solitary hills, or diverging into the grounds of Lady Mary Fleming, his near neighbor, may traverse the deep shades of the woodland, wander along the banks of the rocky rivulet, and finally stand before the well known waterfall there. If he descend into the highway, objects of beauty still present themselves. Cottages and quiet

*From "Homes and Haunts of the Most Eminent British Poets."

ENGLISH LITERARY SHRINES

houses here and there glance from their little spots of Paradise, through the richest boughs of trees; Windermere, with its wide expanse of waters, its fairy islands, its noble hills, allures his steps in one direction; while the sweet little lake of Rydal, with its heronry and its fine background of rocks, invites him in another.

In this direction the vale of Grasmere, the scene of his early married life, opens before him, and Dunmail-raise and Langdale-pikes lift their naked corky summits, as hailing him to the pleasures of old companionship. Into no quarter of this region of lakes, and mountains, and vales of primitive life, can he penetrate without coming upon ground celebrated by his muse. He is truly "sole king of rocky Cumberland."

The immediate grounds in which his house stands are worthy of the country and the man. It is, as its name implies, a mount. Before the house opens a considerable platform, and around and beneath lie various terraces and descend various walks, winding on amid a profusion of trees and luxuriant evergreens. Beyond the house, you ascend various terraces, planted with trees now completely overshadowing them; and these terraces conduct you to a level above the house-top, and extend your view of the enchanting scenery on all sides.

Above yon tower the rocks and precipitous slopes of Nab-scar; and below you, embosomed in its trees, lies the richly ornate villa of Mr. William Ball, a friend, whose family and the poet's are on such social terms, that a little gate between their premises opens both to each family alike. This cottage and grounds were formerly the property of Charles Lloyd, also a friend, and one of the Bristol and Stowey coterie. Both he and Lovell have been long dead; Lovell, indeed, was drowned, on a voyage to Ireland, in the very heyday of the dreams of Pantisocracy, in which he was an eager participant.

The poet's house, itself, is a proper poet's abode. It is at once modest, plain, yet tasteful and elegant. An ordinary dining-room, a breakfast-room in the center, and a library beyond, form the chief apartments. There are a few pictures and busts, especially those of Scott and himself, a good engraving of Burns, and the like, with a good collection of books, few of them very modern.

TWICKENHAM*

BY WILLIAM HOWITT

It seems that Pope did not purchase the freehold of the house and grounds at Twickenham, but only a long lease. He took his father and mother along with him. His father died there the year after, but his mother continued to live till 1733, when she died at the great age of ninety-three. For twenty years she had the singular satisfaction of seeing her son the first poet of his age; carest by the greatest

*From "Homes and Haunts of the Most Eminent British Poets."

men of the time, courted by princes, and feared by all the base. No parents ever found a more tender and dutiful son. With him they shared in honor the ease and distinction he had acquired. They were the cherished objects of his home. Swift paid him no false compliment when he said, in condoling with him on his mother's death, "You are the most dutiful son I have ever known or heard of, which is a felicity not happening to one in a million."

The property at Twickenham is properly described by Roscoe as lying on both sides of the highway, rendering it necessary for him to cross the road to arrive at the higher and more ornamental part of his gardens. In order to obviate this inconvenience, he had recourse to the expedient of excavating a passage under the road from one part of his grounds to the other, a fact to which he alludes in these lines:

"Know all the toil the heavy world can heap,
Rolls o'er my grotto, nor disturbs my sleep."

The lower part of these grounds, in which his house stood, constituted, in fact, only the sloping bank of the river, by much the smaller portion of his territory. The passage, therefore, was very necessary to that far greater part, which was his wilderness, shrubbery, forest, and every thing, where he chiefly planted and worked. This passage he formed into a grotto, having a front of rude stonework opposite to the river and decorated within with spars, ores, and shells. Of this place he has himself left this description:

"I have put the last hand to my works of this kind, in happily finishing the subterranean way and grotto. I found there a spring of the clearest water, which falls in a perpetual rill, that echoes through the cavern night and day. From the River Thames you see through my arch, up a walk of the wilderness, to a kind of open temple wholly composed of shells in the rustic manner; and from that distance under the temple you look down through a sleeping arcade of trees, and see the sails on the river passing suddenly and vanishing, as through a perspective glass. When you shut the door of this grotto, it becomes, on the instant, from a luminous room, a camera obscura, on the walls of which all the objects of the river, hills, woods, and boats are forming a moving picture, in their visible radiations; and when you have a mind to light it less, it affords you a very different scene. It is finished with shells, interspersed with looking-glass in regular forms, and in the ceiling is a star of the same material, at which, when a lamp of an orbicular figure of thin alabaster is hung in the middle, a thousand pointed rays glitter, and are reflected over the place. There are connected to this grotto, by a narrow passage, two porches, one toward the river, of smooth stones full of light and open; the other toward the garden, shadowed with trees, rough with shells, flints, and iron ore. The bottom is paved with simple pebbles, as is also the adjoining walk up the wilderness to the temple, in the natural state, agreeing not ill with the little dripping murmur, and the aquatic idea of the whole place. It wants nothing to complete it but a good statue with an inscription, like that

ENGLISH LITERARY SHRINES

beautiful antique one which you know I am so fond of. You will think I have been very poetical in this description; but it is pretty near the truth."

But it was not merely in forming this grotto that Pope employed himself; it was in building and extending his house, which was in a Roman style, with columns, arcades, and porticos. The designs and elevations of these buildings may be seen by his own hand in the British Museum, drawn in his usual way on backs of letters. The following passage, in a letter to Mr. Digby, will be sufficient to give us his idea of both his Thamesward garden and his house in a summer view: "No ideas you could form in the winter could make you imagine what Twickenham is in this warm summer. Our river glitters beneath the unclouded sun, at the same time that its banks retain the verdure of showers; our gardens are offering their first nosegays; our trees, like new acquaintance brought happily together, are stretching their arms to meet each other, and growing nearer and nearer every hour. The birds are paying their thanksgiving songs for the new habitations I have made them. My building rises high enough to attract the eye and curiosity of the passenger from the river, where, upon beholding a mixture of beauty and ruin, he inquires, 'What house is falling, or what church is arising?' So little taste have our common Tritons for Vitruvius; whatever delight the poetical gods of the river may take in reflecting on their streams, my Tuscan porticos, or Ionic pilasters."

Pope's architecture, like his poetry, has been the subject of much and vehement dispute. On the one hand, his grottos and his buildings have been vituperated as most tasteless and childish; on the other, applauded as beautiful and romantic. Into neither of these disputes need we enter. In both poetry and architecture a bolder spirit and a better taste have prevailed since Pope's time. With all his foibles and defects, Pope was a great poet of the critical and didactic kind, and his house and place had their peculiar beauties. He was himself half inclined to suspect the correctness of his fancy in such matters, and often rallies himself on his gimcracks and crotchets in both verse and prose. . . .

Pope's building madness, however, had method in it. Unlike the great romancer and builder of our time,* he never allowed such things to bring him into debt. He kept his mind at ease by such prudence, and soothed and animated it under circumstances of continued evil by working among his trees, and grottos, and vines, and at his labors of poetry and translations. At the period succeeding the rebellion of 1715, when that event had implicated and scattered so many of his highest and most powerful friends, here he was laboring away at his "Homer" with a progress which astonished every one. Removed at once from the dissipations and distractions of London, and from the agreeable interruptions of such society, he found leisure and health enough here to give him vigor for exertions astonishing for so weak a frame. The tastes he indulged here, if they were not faultless according to our notions, were healthy, and they endured. To the end of his life he preserved his strong attachment to his house and grounds.

*Sir Walter Scott.

V

OTHER ENGLISH SCENES

STONEHENGE*

BY RALPH WALDO EMERSON

We left the train at Salisbury, and took a carriage to Amesbury, passing by Old Sarum, a bare, treeless hill, once containing the town which sent two members to Parliament—now, not a hut—and, arriving at Amesbury, we stopt at the George Inn. After dinner we walked to Salisbury Plain. On the broad downs, under the gray sky, not a house was visible, nothing but Stonehenge, which looked like a group of brown dwarfs in the wide expanse —Stonehenge and the barrows, which rose like green bosses about the plain, and a few hay ricks. On the top of a mountain the old temple would not be more impressive. Far and wide a few shepherds with their flocks sprinkled the plain, and a bagman drove along the road. It looked as if the wide margin given in this crowded isle to this

*From "English Traits." Published by Houghton, Mifflin Co. Emerson's second visit to England, during which he saw Stonehenge, was made in 1847. Of all the Druidical remains in Europe, Stonehenge is perhaps the most remarkable, altho at Carnac in Brittany on the northern shore of the Bay of Biscay, are Druidical remains more numerous, but in general they are smaller and less suggestive of constructive design.

primeval temple were accorded by the veneration of the British race to the old egg out of which all their ecclesiastical structures and history had proceeded.

Stonehenge is a circular colonnade with a diameter of a hundred feet, and enclosing a second and third colonnade within. We walked round the stones, and clambered over them, to wont ourselves with their strange aspect and groupings, and found a nook sheltered from the wind among them, where C.* lighted his cigar. It was pleasant to see that just this simplest of all simple structures—two upright stones and a lintel laid across—had long outstood all later churches, and all history, and were like what is most permanent on the face of the planet: these, and the barrows—(mere mounds of which there are a hundred and sixty within a circle of three miles about Stonehenge)—like the same mound on the plain of Troy, which still makes good to the passing mariner on Hellespont, the vaunt of Homer and the fame of Achilles. Within the enclosure grow buttercups, nettles, and, all around, wild thyme, daisy, meadowsweet, goldenrod, thistle, and the carpeting grass. Over us, larks were soaring and singing—as my friend said: "the larks which were hatched last year, and the wind which was hatched many thousand years ago." We counted and measured by paces the biggest stones, and soon knew as much as any man can suddenly know of the inscrutable temple. There are ninety-four stones, and there were once probably one hundred and sixty. The temple is circular and uncovered, and the situation fixt as-

*Thomas Carlyle, the author of "Sartor Resartus," etc., etc.

OTHER ENGLISH SCENES

tronomically—the grand entrances here, and at Abury, being placed exactly northeast, "as all the gates of the old cavern temples are." How came the stones here, for these sarsens or Druidical sandstones are not found in this neighborhood? The sacrificial stone, as it is called, is the only one in all these blocks that can resist the action of fire, and, as I read in the books, must have been brought one hundred and fifty miles.

On almost every stone we found the marks of the mineralogist's hammer and chisel. The nineteen smaller stones of the inner circle are of granite. I, who had just come from Professor Sedgwick's Cambridge Museum of megatheria and mastodons, was ready to maintain that some cleverer elephants or mylodonta had borne off and laid these rocks one on another. Only the good beasts must have known how to cut a well-wrought tenon and mortise, and to smooth the surface of some of the stones. The chief mystery is, that any mystery should have been allowed to settle on so remarkable a monument, in a country on which all the muses have kept their eyes now for eighteen hundred years. We are not yet too late to learn much more than is known of this structure. Some diligent Fellowes or Layard will arrive, stone by stone, at the whole history, by that exhaustive British sense and perseverance, so whimsical in its choice of objects, which leaves its own Stonehenge or Choir Gaur to the rabbits, while it opens pyramids, and uncovers Nineveh. Stonehenge, in virtue of the simplicity of its plan, and its good preservation, is as if new and recent; and, a thousand years hence, men will thank this age for the accurate history it will yet eliminate.

MAGNA CHARTA ISLAND*

BY MRS. S. C. HALL.

The Company of Basket-makers (if there be such a company) have claimed a large portion of the field—where the barons, "clad in complete steel," assembled to confer with King John upon the great charter of English freedom, by which, Hume truly but coldly says, "very important liabilities and privileges were either granted or secured to every order of men in the kingdom; to the clergy, to the barons, and to the people"—the Basket-makers, we say, have availed themselves of the low land of Runnymead to cultivate osiers; piles and stacks of "withies" in various stages of utility, for several hundred yards shut out the river from the wayfarer, but as he proceeds they disappear, and Cooper's Hill on the left, the rich flat of Runnymead, the Thames, and the groves of time-honored Anckerwycke, on its opposite bank, form together a rich and most interesting picture.

It is now nearly a hundred years since it was first proposed to erect a triumphal column upon Runnymead; but we have sometimes a strange antipathy to do what would seem avoidable; the monument to the memory of Hampden is a sore proof of the niggardliness of liberals to the liberal; but all monuments to such a man or to such a cause must appear poor; the names "Hampden" and "Runnymead" suffice; the green and verdant mead, encircled by the coronet of Cooper's Hill, reposing

*From "Pilgrimages to English Shrines." Magna Charta Island lies in the Thames, a few miles below Windsor.

OTHER ENGLISH SCENES

beneath the sun, and shadowed by the passing cloud, is an object of reverence and beauty, immortalized by the glorious liberty which the bold barons of England forced from a spiritless tyrant.

Tho Cooper's Hill has no claim to the sublimity of mountain scenery, its peculiar situation commands a broad expanse of country. It rises abruptly from the Runnymead meadows, and extends its long ridge in a northwesterly direction; the summit is approached by a winding road, which from different points of the ascent progressively unfolds a gorgeous number of fertile views, such as no other country in the world can give.

"Of hills and dales, and woods, and lawns, and spires,
And glittering towns, and silver streams."

We have heard that the views from Kingswood Lodge—the dwelling of the hill!—are delicious, and that its conservatory contains an exquisite marble statue of "Hope." On the west of Cooper's Hill is the interesting estate of Anckerwycke Purnish. Anckerwycke has been for a series of years in the possession of the family of Harcourt. There is a "meet" of the three shires in this vicinity— Surrey, Buckinghamshire, and Berkshire. The views from the grounds of Anckerwycke are said to be of exceeding beauty, and the kindness of its master makes eloquent the poor about his domain. All these things, and the sound of the rippling waters of the Thames, and the songs of the myriad birds which congregate in its groves, and the legends sprung of its antiquity, all contribute to the adornment of the gigantic fact that here, King John, sorely against his will, signed Magna Charta! How that single fact fills the soul, and nerves the spirit; how proudly the British birthright throbs within our bosoms. We long to lead the new Napoleon, the absolute Nicholas, the frank, hospitable, and brave, but sometimes overconfident American, to this green sward of Runnymead and tell them that here was secured to the Englishman a liberty which other nations have never enjoyed! Here in the thicket beauty of yon little island, was our Charter granted.

There has been much dispute as to whether the Charter was signed upon the Mead or on the island called "Magna Charta Island," which forms a charming feature in the landscape, and upon which is built a little sort of altar-house, so to call it. We leave the settlement of such matters to wiser and more learned heads; but we incline to the idea that John would have felt even the mimic ferry a protection. The island looks even now exclusive, and as we were impelled to its shore, we indulged the belief that the charter was really there signed by the king.

There was a poetic feeling in whoever planted the bank of "Forget-me-not" just at the entrance to the low apartment which was fitted up to contain the charter stone, by the late Simon Harcourt, Esq., in the year 1835. The inscription on the stone is as follows:—"Be it remembered, that on this island, in June, 1215, John, King of England, Signed the Magna Charta, and in the year 1834, this building was erected in commemoration of that great and important event by George Simon Harcourt, Esq., Lord of the Manor and then High

Sheriff of the county." A gentleman rents the island from Mr. Harcourt, and has built there a Gothic cottage in excellent keeping with the place. It adjoins the altar-room, but does not interfere with it, nor with the privileges so graciously bestowed on the public by Mr. Harcourt—permitting patriots or fishermen to visit the island, and picnic in a tent prepared for the purpose, under the shelter of some superb walnut trees.

THE HOME OF THE PILGRIM FATHERS*

BY JAMES M. HOPPIN.

Twelve miles to the south of Doncaster, on the great Northern line of railway, and just at the junction of Yorkshire, Nottinghamshire, and Lincolnshire, in the county of Nottingham, but bordering upon the fenny districts of Lincolnshire, whose monotonous scenery reminds one of Holland, lies the village of Scrooby. Surely it is of more interest to us than all the Pictish forts and Roman walls that the "Laird of Monkbarns" ever dreamed of. I was dropt out of the railway-carriage, which hardly stopt upon a wide plain at a miniature station-house, with some suspicions of a church and small village across the flat rushy fields in the distance. This was indeed the humble village (tho now beginning to be better known) which I had been searching for; and which nobody of whom I inquired in Doncaster, or on the line of the railway, seemed to know anything about,

*From "Old England: Its Scenery, Art and People." Published by Houghton, Mifflin Co.

or even that such a place existed. I made its discovery by the help of a good map. The station-master said he came to Scrooby in 1851, and then it numbered three hundred inhabitants; and since that time there had been but twelve deaths.

My search for the manor-house where Brewster and Bradford established the first church of the Pilgrims, was, for a time, entirely fruitless. I inquired of a genuine "Hodge" working in the fields; but his round red face showed no glimmer of light on the matter so far removed from beans and barley. I next encountered a good Wesleyan minister, trudging his morning circuit of pastoral visitation, but could gain nothing from him, tho a chatty, communicative man. At the venerable stone church of Scrooby, very rude and plain in architecture, but by no means devoid of picturesqueness, I was equally unsuccessful. The verger of the church, who is generally the learned man of the village, was absent; and his daughter knew nothing outside the church and churchyard.

I strolled along the grassy country road that ran through the place till I met a white-haired old countryman, who proved to be the most intelligent soul in the neighborhood. He put his cane to his chin, shut and opened his eyes, and at last told me in broad Yorkshire, that he thought the place I was looking for must be what they called "the bishop's house," where Squire Dickinson lived. Set at last upon the right track, I walked across two swampy meadows that bordered the Idle River—pertinently named—till I came to a solitary farmhouse with a red-tiled roof. Some five or six slender poplar-trees stood at the back of it, and a ditch of water at one end, where there had been evidently an ancient moat—"a moated grange."

It was a desolate spot, and was rendered more so just then by the coming up of a thunder-storm, whose "avant courier," the wind, made the slender poplars and osiers bend and twist. Squire John Dickinson, the present inhabitant of the house, which is owned by Richard Monckton Milnes, the poet, gave me a hearty farmer's welcome. I think he said there had been one other American there before; at any rate he had an inkling that he was squatted on soil of some peculiar interest to Americans. He introduced me to his wife and daughters, healthy and rosy-cheeked English women, and made me sit down to a hospitable luncheon. He entertained me with a discourse upon the great amount of hard work to be done in farming among these bogs, and wished he had never undertaken it, but had gone to America or Australia. The house, he said, was rickety enough, but he contrived to make it do. It was, he thought, principally made of what was once a part of the stable of the Manor House.

The palace itself has now entirely disappeared; "but," said my host, "dig anywhere around here and you will find the ruins of the old palace." Dickinson said that he himself was reared in Austerfield, a few miles off in Yorkshire; and that a branch of the Bradford family still lived there. After luncheon I was shown Cardinal Wolsey's mulberry-tree, or what remained of it; and in one of the barns, some elaborately carved woodwork and ornamental beams, covered with dirt and cobwebs, were pointed out, which undoubtedly belonged to the archiepiscopal palace.

This was all that remained of the house where Elder Brewster once lived, and gathered his humble friends about him, in a simple form of worship. . . . This manor was assigned to the Archbishop of York in the "Doomsday Book." Cardinal Wolsey, when he held that office, passed some time at this palace. While he lived there, Henry VIII. slept a night in the house. It came into Archbishop Sandys's hands in 1576. He gave it by lease to his son, Samuel Sandys, under whom Brewster held the manor. Brewster, as is now well known, was the Post-Superintendent of Scrooby, an important position in those days, lying as the village did, and does now, upon the great northern line of travel from London to Yorkshire, Northumberland, and Scotland. . . .

But to look at this lonely and decayed manor-house, standing in the midst of these flat and desolate marshes, and at this most obscure village of the land, this Nazareth of England, slumbering in rustic ignorance and stupid apathy, and to think of what has come out of this place, of what vast influences and activities have issued from this quiet and almost listless scene, one has strange feelings. The storied "Alba Longa," from which Rome sprang, is an interesting spot, but the newly discovered spiritual birthplace of America may excite deeper emotions.

OTHER ENGLISH SCENES

OXFORD*

BY GOLDWIN SMITH

There is in Oxford much that is not as old as it looks. The buildings of the Bodleian Library, University College, Oriel, Exeter, and some others, medieval or half medieval in their style, are Stuart in date. In Oxford the Middle Ages lingered long. Yon cupola of Christ Church is the work of Wren, yon towers of All Souls' are the work of a still later hand. The Headington stone, quickly growing black and crumbling, gives the buildings a false hue of antiquity. An American visitor, misled by the blackness of University College, remarked to his host that the buildings must be immensely old. "No," replied his host, "their color deceives you; their age is not more than two hundred years." It need not be said that Palladian edifices like Queen's, or the new buildings of Magdalen, are not the work of a Chaplain of Edward III., or a Chancellor of Henry VI. But of the University buildings, St. Mary's Church and the Divinity School, of the College buildings, the old quadrangles of Merton, New College, Magdalen, Brasenose, and detached pieces not a few are genuine Gothic of the Founders' age.

Here are six centuries, if you choose to include the Norman castle, here are eight centuries, and, if you choose to include certain Saxon remnants in Christ Church Cathedral, here are ten centuries, chronicled in stone. Of the corporate lives of these Colleges, the threads

*From "Oxford and Her Colleges." By arrangement with the publishers, Macmillan Co. Copyright, 1893.

have run unbroken through all the changes and revolutions, political, religious, and social, between the Barons' War and the present hour. The economist goes to their muniment rooms for the record of domestic management and expenditure during those ages.

Till yesterday, the codes of statutes embodying their domestic law, tho largely obsolete, remained unchanged. Nowhere else in England, at all events, unless it be at the sister University, can the eye and mind feed upon so much antiquity, certainly not upon so much antique beauty, as on the spot where we stand. That all does not belong to the same remote antiquity, adds to the interest and to the charm. This great home of learning, with its many architectures, has been handed from generation to generation, each generation making its own improvements, impressing its own tastes, embodying its own tendencies, down to the present hour. It is like a great family mansion, which owner after owner has enlarged or improved to meet his own needs or tastes, and which, thus chronicling successive phases of social and domestic life, is wanting in uniformity but not in living interest or beauty.

Oxford is a federation of Colleges. It had been strictly so for two centuries, and every student had been required to be a member of a college when, in 1856, non-collegiate students, of whom there are now a good many, were admitted. The University is the federal government. The Chancellor, its nominal head, is a non-resident grandee, usually a political leader whom the University delights to honor and whose protection it desires. Only on great state occasions does he appear in

OTHER ENGLISH SCENES

his gown richly embroidered with gold. The acting chief is the Vice-Chancellor, one of the heads of Colleges, who marches with the Bedel carrying the mace before him, and has been sometimes taken by strangers for the attendant of the Bedel. With him are the two Proctors, denoted by their velvet sleeves, named by the Colleges in turn, the guardians of University discipline.

The University Legislature consists of three houses—an elective Council, made up equally of heads of Colleges, professors, and Masters of Arts; the Congregation of residents, mostly teachers of the University or Colleges; and the Convocation, which consists of all Masters of Arts, resident or non-resident, if they are present to vote. Congregation numbers 400, Convocation nearly 6,000. Legislation is initiated by the Council, and has to make its way through Convocation and Congregation, with some chance of being wrecked between the academical Congregation, which is progressive, and the rural Convocation, which is conservative. The University regulates the general studies, holds all the examinations, except that at entrance, which is held by the Colleges, confers all the degrees and honors, and furnishes the police of the academical city. Its professors form the general and superior staff of teachers. Each College, at the same time, is a little polity in itself. It has its own governing body, consisting of a Head (President, Master, Principal, Provost, or Warden) and a body of Fellows. It holds its own estates; noble estates, some of them are. It has its private staff of teachers or tutors, usually taken from the Fellows, tho the subjects of teaching are those recognized by the University examinations. . . .

SEEING EUROPE WITH FAMOUS AUTHORS

The buildings of the University lie mainly in the center of the city around us. There is the Convocation House, the hall of the University Legislature, where, in times of collision between theological parties, or between the party of the ancient system of education and that of the modern system, lively debates have been heard. In it, also, are conferred the ordinary degrees. They are still conferred in the religious form of words, handed down from the Middle Ages, the candidate kneeling down before the Vice-Chancellor in the posture of medieval homage. Oxford is the classic ground of old forms and ceremonies. Before each degree is conferred, the Proctors march up and down the House to give any objector to the degree—an unsatisfied creditor, for example—the opportunity of entering a caveat by "plucking" the Proctor's sleeve. Adjoining the Convocation House is the Divinity School, the only building of the University, saving St. Mary's Church, which dates from the Middle Ages. A very beautiful relic of the Middle Ages it is when seen from the gardens of Exeter College. Here are held the examinations for degrees in theology, styled, in Oxford of old, queen of the sciences, and long their tyrant. Here, again, is the Sheldonian Theater, the gift of Archbishop Sheldon, a Primate of the Restoration period, and as readers of Pepys's "Diary" know, of Restoration character, but a patron of learning. . . .

The Clarendon was built with the proceeds of the history written by the Minister of the early Restoration, who was Chancellor of the University, and whose touching letter of farewell to her, on his fall and flight from England, may be seen

OTHER ENGLISH SCENES

in the Bodleian Library. There, also, are preserved documents which may help to explain his fall. They are the written dialogs which passed between him and his master at the board of the Privy Council, and they show that Clarendon, having been the political tutor of Charles the exile, too much bore himself as the political tutor of Charles the king. In the Clarendon are the University Council Chamber and the Registry. Once it was the University press, but the press has now a far larger mansion yonder to the northwest, whence, besides works of learning and science, go forth Bibles and prayer-books in all languages to all quarters of the globe. Legally, as a printer of Bibles the University has a privilege, but its real privilege is that which it secures for itself by the most scrupulous accuracy and by infinitesimal profits.

Close by is the University Library, the Bodleian, one of those great libraries of the world in which you can ring up at a few minutes' notice almost any author of any age or country. This Library is one of those entitled by law to a copy of every book printed in the United Kingdom, and it is bound to preserve all that it receives, a duty which might in the end burst any building, were it not that the paper of many modern books is happily perishable. . . . We stand in the Radcliffe, formerly the medical and physical library, now a supplement and an additional reading-room of the Bodleian, the gift of Dr. Radcliffe, Court Physician and despot of the profession in the times of William and Anne, of whose rough sayings, and sayings more than rough, some are preserved in his "Life." He it was who told William III. that he would not have His Majesty's two legs for his three kingdoms, and who is said to have punished the giver of a niggardly fee by a prediction of death, which was fulfilled by the terrors of the patient. Close at hand is the Ashmolean, the old University Museum, now only a museum of antiquities, the most precious of which is King Alfred's gem. Museum and Medical Library have together migrated to the new edifice on the north side of the city.

But of all the University buildings the most beautiful is St. Mary's Church, where the University sermons are preached, and from the pulpit of which, in the course of successive generations and successive controversies, a changeful and often heady current of theology has flowered. There preached Newman, Pusey, and Manning; there preached Hampden, Stanley, and the authors of "Essays and Reviews." . . .

On the north of the city, where fifty years ago stretched green fields, is now seen a suburb of villas, all of them bespeaking comfort and elegance, few of them overweening wealth. These are largely the monuments of another great change, the removal of the rule of celibacy from the Fellowships, and the introduction of a large body of married teachers devoted to their profession, as well as of the revival of the Professorships, which were always tenable by married men. Fifty years ago the wives of Heads of Houses, who generally married late in life if they married at all, constituted, with one or two officers of the University, the whole female society of Oxford. The change was inevitable, if education was to be made a profession, instead of being,

OTHER ENGLISH SCENES

as it had been in the hands of celibate Fellows of Colleges, merely the transitory occupation of a man whose final destination was the parish. Those who remember the old Common Room life, which is now departing, can not help looking back with a wistful eye to its bachelor ease, its pleasant companionship, its interesting talk and free interchange of thought, its potations neither "deep" nor "dull."

Nor were its symposia without important fruits when such men as Newman and Ward, on one side, encountered such men as Whateley, Arnold, and Tait, on the other side in Common Room talk over great questions of the day. But the life became dreary when a man had passed forty, and it is well exchanged for the community that fills those villas, and which, with its culture, its moderate and tolerably equal incomes, permitting hospitality but forbidding luxury, and its unity of interests with its diversity of acquirements and accomplishments, seems to present the ideal conditions of a pleasant social life. The only question is, how the College system will be maintained when the Fellows are no longer resident within the walls of the College to temper and control the younger members, for a barrack of undergraduates is not a good thing. The personal bond and intercourse between Tutor and pupil under the College system was valuable as well as pleasant; it can not be resigned without regret. But its loss will be compensated by far superior teaching.

SEEING EUROPE WITH FAMOUS AUTHORS

CAMBRIDGE*

BY JAMES M. HOPPIN.

I was struck with the positive resemblances between Oxford and Cambridge. Both are situated on slightly rising ground, with broad green meadows and a flat, fenny country stretching around them. The winding and muddy Cam, holding the city in its arm, might be easily taken for the fond but still more capricious Isis, tho both of them are insignificant streams; and Jesus' College Green and Midsummer Common at Cambridge, correspond to Christ Church Meadows and those bordering the Cherwell at Oxford. At a little distance, the profile of Cambridge is almost precisely like that of Oxford, while glorious King's College Chapel makes up all deficiencies in the architectural features and outline of Cambridge.

Starting from Bull Inn, we will not linger long in the streets, tho we might be tempted to do so by the luxurious book-shops, but will make straight for the gateway of Trinity College. This gateway is itself a venerable and imposing structure, altho a mass of houses clustered about it destroys its unity with the rest of the college buildings. Between its two heavy battlemented towers are a statue of Edward III. and his coat-of-arms; and over the gate Sir Isaac Newton had his observatory.

This gateway introduces into a noble court, called the Great Court, with a carved stone fountain or canopied well in the center, and buildings of ir-

*From "Old England: Its Scenery, Art and People." Published by Houghton, Mifflin Co.

OTHER ENGLISH SCENES

regular sizes and different ages inclosing it. The chapel which forms the northern side of this court dates back to 1564. In the ante-chapel, or vestibule, stands the statue of Sir Isaac Newton, by Roubiliac. It is spirited, but, like all the works of this artist, unnaturally attenuated. The head is compact rather than large, and the forehead square rather than high. The face has an expression of abstract contemplation, and is looking up, as if the mind were just fastening upon the beautiful law of light which is suggested by the hand holding a prism. By the door of the screen entering into the chapel proper, are the sitting statues of Sir Francis Bacon and Dr. Isaac Barrow, two more giants of this college. The former represents the philosopher in a sitting posture, wearing his high-crowned hat, and leaning thoughtfully upon his hand.

The hall of Trinity College, which separates the Great Court from the Inner or Neville Court, (courts in Cambridge, quads in Oxford), is the glory of the college. Its interior is upward of one hundred feet in length, oak-wainscoted, with deep beam-work ceiling, now black with age, and an enormous fireplace, which in winter still blazes with its old hospitable glow. At the upper end where the professors and fellows sit, hang the portraits of Bacon and Newton. I had the honor of dining in this most glorious of banqueting-halls, at the invitation of a fellow of the college. Before meals, the ancient Latin grace, somewhat abbreviated, is pronounced.

We pass through the hall into Neville Court, three sides of which are cloistered, and in the eastern end of which stands the fine library building, built through the exertions of Dr. Barrow, who was determined that nothing in Oxford should surpass his own darling college. The library room is nearly two hundred feet long, with tesselated marble floor, and with the busts of the great men of Trinity ranged around the walls. The wood-carvings of Grinling Gibbons that adorn this room, of flowers, fruit, wheat, grasshoppers, birds, are of singular beauty, and make the hard oak fairly blossom and live. This library contains the most complete collection of the various editions of Shakespeare's Works which exists. Thorwaldsen's statue of Byron, who was a student of this college, stands at the south end of the room. It represents him in the bloom of youth, attired as a pilgrim, with pencil in hand and a broken Grecian column at his feet. . . .

The next neighbor to Trinity on the north, and the next in point of size and importance in the University, is St. John's College. It has four courts, one opening into the other. It also is jealously surrounded by high walls, and its entrance is by a ponderous old tower, having a statue of St. John the Evangelist over the gateway. Through a covered bridge, not unlike "the Bridge of Sighs," one passes over the stream to a group of modern majestic castellated buildings of yellow stone belonging to this college. The grounds, walks, and thick groves connected with this building form an elegant academic shade, and tempt to a life of exclusive study and scholarly accumulation, of growing fat in learning, without perhaps growing muscular in the effort to use it. . . .

King's College, founded by Henry VII., from

OTHER ENGLISH SCENES

whom it takes its name, comes next in order. Its wealthy founder, who, like his son, loved architectural pomp, had great designs in regard to this institution, which were cut off by his death, but the massive unfinished gateway of the old building stands as a regal specimen of what the whole plan would have been had it been carried out. Henry VIII., however, perfected some of his father's designs on a scale of true magnificence. King's College Chapel, the glory of Cambridge and England, is in the perpendicular style of English Gothic. It is three hundred and sixteen feet long, eighty-four feet broad, its sides ninety feet, and its tower one hundred and forty-six feet high. Its lofty interior stone roof in the fan-tracery form of groined ceiling has the appearance of being composed of immense white scallop-shells, with heavy corbels of rich flowers and bunches of grapes suspended at their points of junction. The ornamental emblem of the Tudor rose and portcullis is carved in every conceivable spot and nook. Twenty-four stately and richly painted windows, divided into the strong vertical lines of the Perpendicular style, and crossed at right angles by lighter transoms and more delicate circular moldings, with the great east and west windows flashing in the most vivid and superb colors, make it a gorgeous vision of light and glory. . . .

On the same street, and nearly opposite St. Peter's, is Pembroke College, a most interesting and venerable pile, with a quaint gable front. Its buildings are small, and it is said, for some greatly needed city improvement, will probably be soon torn down; on hearing which, I thought, would that some genius like Aladdin's, or some angel who bore through the air the chapel of the "Lady of Loretto," might bear these old buildings bodily to our land and set them down on the Yale grounds, so that we might exchange their picturesque antiquity for the present college buildings, which, tho endeared to us by many associations, are like a row of respectable brick factories.

Edmund Spenser and William Pitt belonged to Pembroke; and Gray, the poet, driven from St. Peter's by the pranks and persecutions of his fellow students, spent the remainder of his university life here. Some of the cruel, practical jokes inflicted upon the timid and delicate nature sound like the modern days of "hazing freshmen." Among his other fancies and fears, Gray was known to be especially afraid of fire, and kept always coiled up in his room a rope-ladder, in case of emergency. By a preconcerted signal, on a dark winter night, a tremendous cry of fire was raised in the court below, which caused the young poet to leap out of bed and to hastily descend his rope-ladder into a mighty tub of ice-cold water, set for that purpose. . . .

Sidney Sussex and Imanuel Colleges were called by Archbishop Laud "the nurseries of Puritanism." The college-book of Sidney Sussex contains this record: "Oliver Cromwell of Huntingdon was admitted as an associate on the 26th day of April, 1616. Tutor Richard Howlet." He had just completed his seventeenth year. Cromwell's father dying the next year, and leaving but a small estate, the young "Protector" was obliged to leave college for more practical pursuits. "But some Latin," Bishop Burnett said, "stuck to him." An oriel window looking upon Bridge Street, is

OTHER ENGLISH SCENES

pointed out as marking his room; and in the master's lodge is a likeness of Cromwell in his later years, said to be the best extant. The gray hair is parted in the middle of the forehead, and hangs down long upon the shoulders, like that of Milton. The forehead is high and swelling, with a deep line sunk between the eyes. The eyes are gray. The complexion is florid and mottled, and all the features rugged and large. Heavy, corrugated furrows of decision and resolute will are plowed about the mouth, and the lips are shut like a vice. Otherwise, the face has a calm and benevolent look, not unlike that of Benjamin Franklin.

In Sidney Sussex, Cromwell's College, and in two or three other colleges of Cambridge University, we find the head-sources of English Puritanism, which, in its best form, was no wild and unenlightened enthusiasm, but the product of thoughtful and educated minds. We shall come soon upon the name of Milton. John Robinson, our national father, and the Moses of our national exodus, as well as Elder Brewster, John Cotton and many others of the principal Puritan leaders and divines, were educated at Cambridge. Sir Henry Vane, the younger, whom Macintosh regarded as not inferior to Bacon in depth of intellect, and to whom Milton addrest the sonnet, who was chosen Governor of Massachusetts, and who infused much of his own thoughtful and profound spirit into Puritan institutions at home and in America, was a student of Magdalen College, Oxford.

A little further on to the south of Sidney Sussex, upon St. Andrew's Street, is Christ's College. The front and gate are old; the other buildings are after a design by Inigo Jones. In the garden stands the famous mulberry-tree said to have been planted by Milton. It is still vigorous, tho carefully propt up and mounded around, and its aged trunk is sheathed with lead. The martyr Latimer, John Howe, the prince of theological writers, and Archdeacon Paley, belonged to this college; but its most brilliant name is that of John Milton. He entered in 1624; took the degree of Bachelor of Arts in 1628, and that of Master of Arts in 1632. This is the entry in the college record: "John Milton of London, son of John Milton, was entered as a student in the elements of letters under Master Hill of the Pauline School, February 12, 1624. . . ." Milton has indignantly defended himself against the slander of his political enemies, that he left college in disgrace, and calls it "a commodious lie." . . .

It is noticeable that Cambridge has produced all the great poets; Oxford, with her yearnings and strivings, none. Milton were glory enough; but Spenser, Gray, Byron, Coleridge, Wordsworth, Tennyson (a Lincolnshire man), may be thrown in. It might be said of Cambridge, as Dr. Johnson said of Pembroke College, "We are a nest of singing birds here." Milton, from the extreme elegance of his person and his mind, rather than from any effeminateness of character, was called while in the University, "the lady of Christ's College." The young poet could not have been inspired by outward Nature in his own room; for the miniature dormer-windows are too high to look out of at all. It is a small attic chamber, with very steep narrow stairs leading up to it. The name of "Milton" (so it is said to be, tho hard to make out) is cut in the old oaken door.

OTHER ENGLISH SCENES

CHESTER*

BY NATHANIEL HAWTHORNE.

I went with Mr. Ticknor to Chester by railway. It is quite an indescribable old town, and I feel as if I had had a glimpse of old England. The wall encloses a large space within the town, but there are numerous houses and streets not included within its precincts. Some of the principal streets pass under the ancient gateways; and at the side there are flights of steps, giving access to the summit. Around the top of the whole wall, a circuit of about two miles, there runs a walk, well paved with flagstones, and broad enough for three persons to walk abreast. . . .

The most utterly indescribable feature of Chester is the Rows, which every traveler has attempted to describe. At the height of several feet above some of the oldest streets, a walk runs through the front of the houses, which project over it. Back of the walk there are shops; on the outer side is a space of two or three yards, where the shopmen place their tables, and stands, and show-cases; overhead, just high enough for persons to stand erect, a ceiling. At frequent intervals little narrow passages go winding in among the houses, which all along are closely conjoined, and seem to have no access or exit, except through the shops, or into these narrow passages, where you can touch each side with your elbows, and the top with your

*From "English Note-Books." By special arrangement with, and by permission of, the publishers, Houghton, Mifflin Co. Copyright, 1870-1898.

OTHER ENGLISH SCENES

hand. We penetrated into one or two of them, and they smelt anciently and disagreeably.

At one of the doors stood a pale-looking, but cheerful and good-natured woman, who told us that she had come to that house when first married, 21 years before, and had lived there ever since; and that she felt as if she had been buried through the best years of her life. She allowed us to peep into her kitchen and parlor—small, dingy, dismal, but yet not wholly destitute of a home look. She said she had seen two or three coffins in a day, during cholera times, carried out of that narrow passage into which her door opened. These avenues put me in mind of those which run through ant-hills, or those which a mole makes underground. This fashion of Rows does not appear to be going out; and, for aught I can see, it may last hundreds of years longer. When a house becomes so old as to be untenantable, it is rebuilt, and the new one is fashioned like the old, so far as regards the walk runnng through its front. Many of the shops are very good, and even elegant, and these Rows are the favorite places of business in Chester. Indeed, they have many advantages, the passengers being sheltered from the rain, and there being within the shops that dimmer light by which tradesmen like to exhibit their wares.

A large proportion of the edifices in the Rows must be comparatively modern; but there are some very ancient ones, with oaken frames visible on the exterior. The Row, passing through these houses, is railed with oak, so old that it has turned black, and grown to be as hard as stone, which it might be mistaken for, if one did not see where names and initials have been cut into it with knives at

OTHER ENGLISH SCENES

some bygone period. Overhead, cross-beams project through the ceiling so low as almost to hit the head. On the front of one of these buildings was the inscription, "God's Providence is mine Inheritance," said to have been put there by the occupant of the house two hundred years ago, when the plague spared this one house only in the whole city. Not improbably the inscription has operated as a safeguard to prevent the demolition of the house hitherto; but a shopman of an adjacent dwelling told us that it was soon to be taken down.

Here and there, about some of the streets through which the Rows do not run, we saw houses of very aged aspect, with steep, peaked gables. The front gable-end was supported on stone pillars, and the sidewalk passed beneath. Most of these old houses seemed to be taverns,—the Black Bear, the Green Dragon, and such names. We thought of dining at one of them, but, on inspection, they looked rather too dingy and close, and of questionable neatness. So we went to the Royal Hotel, where we probably fared just as badly at much more expense, and where there was a particularly gruff and crabbed old waiter, who, I suppose, thought himself free to display his surliness because we arrived at the hotel on foot. For my part, I love to see John Bull show himself. I must go again and again and again to Chester, for I suppose there is not a more curious place in the world.

SEEING EUROPE WITH FAMOUS AUTHORS

EDDYSTONE LIGHTHOUSE*

BY FREDERICK A. TALBOT.

It is doubtful whether the name of any lighthouse is so familiar throughout the English-speaking world as the "Eddystone." Certainly no other "pillar of fire by night, of cloud by day," can offer so romantic a story of dogged engineering perseverance, of heartrending disappointments, disaster, blasted hopes, and brilliant success.

Standing out in the English Channel, about sixty miles east of the Lizard, is a straggling ridge of rocks which stretches for hundreds of yards across the marine thoroughfare, and also obstructs the western approach to Plymouth Harbor. But at a point some nine and a half miles south of Rame Head on the mainland the reef rises somewhat abruptly to the surface, so that at low-water two or three ugly granite knots are bared, which tell only too poignantly the complete destruction they could wreak upon a vessel which had the temerity or the ill luck to scrape over them at high-tide. Even in the calmest weather the sea curls and eddies viciously around these stones; hence the name "Eddystone," is derived. . . .

As British overseas traffic expanded, the idea of indicating the spot for the benefit of vessels was discust. The first practical suggestion was put forward about the year 1664, but thirty-two years elapsed before any attempt was made to reduce theory to practise. Then an eccentric English country gentleman, Henry Winstanley, who dabbled

---

*From "Lightships and Lighthouses." Courtesy of J. B. Lippincott Co., the publishers.

OTHER ENGLISH SCENES

in mechanical engineering upon unorthodox lines, came forward and offered to build a lighthouse upon the terrible rocks. Those who knew this ambitious amateur were dubious of his success, and wondered what manifestation his eccentricity would assume on this occasion. Nor was their scepticism entirely misplaced. Winstanley raised the most fantastic lighthouse which has ever been known, and which would have been more at home in a Chinese cemetery than in the English Channel. It was wrought in wood and most lavishly embellished with carvings and gilding.

Four years were occupied in its construction, and the tower was anchored to the rock by means of long, heavy irons. The light, merely a flicker, flashed out from this tower in 1699, and for the first time the proximity of the Eddystones was indicated all around the horizon by night. Winstanley's critics were rather free in expressing their opinion that the tower would come down with the first sou'wester, but the eccentric builder was so intensely proud of his invention as to venture the statement that it would resist the fiercest gale that ever blew, and, when such did occur, he hoped that he might be in the tower at the time.

Fate gratified his wish, for while he was on the rock in the year 1703 one of the most terrible tempests that ever have assailed the coasts of Britain gript the structure, tore it up by the roots, and hurled it into the Channel, where it was battered to pieces, its designer and five keepers going down with the wreck. When the inhabitants of Plymouth, having vainly scanned the horizon for a sign of the tower on the following morning, put off to the rock to investigate, they found only the bent and twisted iron rods by which the tower had been held in position projecting mournfully into the air from the rock-face.

Shortly after the demolition of the tower, the reef, as if enraged at having been denied a number of victims owing to the existence of the warning light, trapt the "Winchelsea" as she was swinging up Channel, and smashed her to atoms, with enormous loss of life.

Altho the first attempt to conquer the Eddystone had terminated so disastrously, it was not long before another effort was made to mark the reef. The builder this time was a Cornish laborer's son, John Rudyerd, who had established himself in business on Ludgate Hill as a silk mercer. In his youth he had studied civil engineering, but his friends had small opinion of his abilities in this craft. However, he attacked the problem boldly, and, altho his tower was a plain, business-looking structure, it would have been impossible to conceive a design capable of meeting the peculiar requirements of the situation more efficiently. It was a cone, wrought in timber, built upon a stone and wood foundation anchored to the rock, and of great weight and strength. The top of the cone was cut off to permit the lantern to be set in position. The result was that externally the tower resembled the trunk of an oak tree, and appeared to be just about as strong. It offered the minimum of resistance to the waves, which, tumbling upon the ledge, rose and curled around the tapering form without starting a timber.

For forty years Rudyerd's structure defied the elements, and probably would have been standing to this day had it not possest one weak point.

OTHER ENGLISH SCENES

It was built of wood instead of stone. Consequently, when a fire broke out in the lantern on December 4, 1755, the flames, fanned by the breeze, rapidly made their way downward.

No time was lost in erecting another tower on the rock, for now it was more imperative than ever that the reef should be lighted adequately. The third engineer was John Smeaton, who first landed on the rock to make the surveys on April 5, 1756. He was able to stay there for only two and a quarter hours before the rising tide drove him off, but in that brief period he had completed the work necessary to the preparation of his design. Wood had succumbed to the attacks of tempest and of fire in turn.

Smeaton would use material which would defy both—Portland stone. He also introduced a slight change in the design for such structures, and one which has been universally copied, producing the graceful form of lighthouse with which everyone is so familiar. Instead of causing the sides to slope upward in the straight lines of a cone, such as Rudyerd adopted, Smeaton preferred a slightly concave curve, so that the tower was given a waist about half its height. He also selected the oak tree as his guide, but one having an extensive spread of branches, wherein will be found a shape in the trunk, so far as the broad lines are concerned, which coincides with the form of Smeaton's lighthouse. He chose a foundation where the rock shelved gradually to its highest point, and dropt vertically into the water upon the opposite side. The face of the rock was roughly trimmed to permit the foundation stones of the tower to be laid. The base of the building was perfectly solid to the entrance level, and each stone was dovetailed securely into its neighbor.

From the entrance, which was about 15 feet above high water, a central well, some five feet in diameter, containing a staircase, led to the storeroom, nearly 30 feet above high water. Above this was a second storeroom, a living-room as the third floor, and the bedroom beneath the lantern. The light was placed about 72 feet above high water, and comprised a candelabra having two rings, one smaller than and placed within the other, but raised about a foot above its level, the two being held firmly in position by means of chains suspended from the roof and secured to the floor. The rings were adapted to receive twenty-four lights, each candle weighing about two and three-quarter ounces. Even candle manufacture was in its infancy in those days, and periodically the keepers had to enter the lantern to snuff the wicks. In order to keep the watchers of the lights on the alert, Smeaton installed a clock of the grandfather pattern in the tower, and fitted it with a gong, which struck every half hour to apprise the men of these duties. This clock is now one of the most interesting relics in the museum at Trinity House.* . . .

The lighthouse had been standing for 120 years when ominous reports were received by the Trinity Brethren concerning the stability of the tower. The keepers stated that during severe storms the building shook alarmingly. A minute inspection

*Trinity House, an association founded in London in 1512-1514, is "empowered by charter to examine, license and regulate pilots, to erect beacons and lighthouses, and to place buoys in channels and rivers."

OTHER ENGLISH SCENES

of the structure was made, and it was found that, altho the work of Smeaton's masons was above reproach, time and weather had left their mark. The tower itself was becoming decrepit. The binding cement had decayed, and the air imprisoned and comprest within the interstices by the waves was disintegrating the structure slowly but surely.

Under these circumstances it was decided to build a new tower on another convenient ledge, forming part of the main reef, about 120 feet distant. Sir James Douglass, the engineer-in-chief to Trinity House, completed the designs and personally superintended their execution. The Smeaton lines were taken as a basis, with one important exception. Instead of a curve commencing at the foundation, the latter comprized a perfect cylindrical monolith of masonry 22 feet in height by 44 feet in diameter. From this basis the tower springs to a height which brings the local plane 130 feet above the highest spring tides. The top of the base is 30 inches above high water, and, the tower's diameter being less than that of its plinth, the set-off forms an excellent landing-stage when the weather permits.

The site selected for the Douglass tower being lower than that chosen by Smeaton, the initial work was more exacting, as the duration of the working period was reduced. The rock, being gneiss, was extremely tough, and the preliminary quarrying operations for the foundation stones which had to be sunk into the rock were tedious and difficult, especially as the working area was limited. Each stone was dovetailed, not only to its neighbor on either side, but below and above as well. The foundation stones were dovetailed into the reef and were secured still further by the aid of tow bolts, each one and a half inches in diameter, which were passed through the stone and sunk deeply into the rock below. . . .

The tower has eight floors, exclusive of the entrance; there are two oil rooms, one above the other, holding 4,300 gallons of oil, above which is a coal and store room, followed by a second storeroom. Outside the tower at this level is a crane, by which supplies are hoisted, and which also facilitates the landing and embarkation of the keepers, who are swung through the air in a stirrup attached to the crane rope. Then, in turn, come the living-room, the "low light" room, bedroom, service room, and finally the lantern. For the erection of the tower, 2,171 blocks of granite, which were previously fitted temporarily in their respective positions on shore and none of which weighed less than two tons, were used. When the work was commenced, the engineer estimated that the task would occupy five years, but on May 18, 1882, the lamp was lighted by the Duke of Edinburgh, the Master of Trinity House at the time, the enterprise having occupied only four years. Some idea may thus be obtained of the energy with which the labor was prest forward, once the most trying sections were overcome. . . .

When the new tower was completed and brought into service, the Smeaton building was demolished. This task was carried out with extreme care, inasmuch as the citizens of Plymouth had requested that the historic Eddystone structure might be erected on Plymouth Hoe, on the spot occupied by the existing Trinity House landmark. The authorities agreed to this proposal, and the ownership of the Smeaton tower was forthwith transferred to the people of Plymouth. But demolition was carried out only to the level of Smeaton's lower storeroom. The staircase, well, and entrance were filled up with masonry, the top was beveled off, and in the center of the stump an iron pole was planted. While the Plymouth Hoe relic is but one-half of the tower, its reerection was completed faithfully, and, moreover, carries the original candelabra which the famous engineer devised.

Not only is the Douglass tower a beautiful example of lighthouse engineering, but it was relatively cheap. The engineer, when he prepared the designs, estimated that an outlay of £78,000, or $390,000, would be incurred. As a matter of fact, the building cost only £59,255, or $296,275, and a saving of £18,000, or $90,000, in a work of this magnitude is no mean achievement. All things considered, the Eddystone is one of the cheapest sea-rock lights which has ever been consummated.

THE CAPITAL OF THE BRITISH, SAXON AND NORMAN KINGS*

BY WILLIAM HOWITT

What an interesting old city is Winchester! and how few people are aware of it! The ancient capital of the kingdom—the capital of the British, and the Saxon, and the Norman kings—the favorite resort of our kings and queens, even till the revolution of 1688; the capital which, for ages, main-

*From "Visits to Remarkable Places."

tained a proud, and long a triumphant, rivalry with London itself; the capital which once boasted upward of ninety churches and chapels, whose meanest houses now stand upon the foundations of noble palaces and magnificent monasteries; and in whose ruins or in whose yet superb minster lie enshrined the bones of mighty kings, and fair and pious queens; of lordly abbots and prelates, who in their day swayed not merely the destinies of this one city, but of the kingdom. There she sits—a sad, discrowned queen, and how few are acquainted with her in the solitude of her desertion! Yet where is the place, saving London itself, which can compete with her in solemn and deep interest? Where is the city, except that, in Great Britain, which can show so many objects of antique beauty, or call up so many national recollections?

Here lie the bones of Alfred—here he was probably born, for this was at that time the court and the residence of his parents. Here, at all events, he spent his infancy and the greater portion of his youth. Here he imbibed the wisdom and the magnanimity of mind with which he afterward laid the foundations of our monarchy, our laws, liberties and literature, and in a word, of our national greatness.

Hence Alfred went forth to fight those battles which freed his country from the savage Dane; and, having done more for his realm and race than ever monarch did before or since, here he lay down, in the strength of his years, and consigned his tomb as a place of grateful veneration to a people whose future greatness even his sagacious spirit could not be prophetic enough to foresee.

OTHER ENGLISH SCENES

Were it only for the memory and tomb of this great king, Winchester ought to be visited by every Englishman with the most profound veneration and affection; but here also lie the ashes of nearly all Alfred's family and kin: his father Ethelwolf, who saw the virtues and talents, and prognosticated the greatness of his son; his noble-minded mother, who breathed into his infant heart the most sublime sentiments; his royal brothers, and his sons and daughters. Here also repose Canute, who gave that immortal reproof on the Southampton shore to his sycophantic courtiers, and his celebrated queen Emma, so famous at once for her beauty and her trials. Here is still seen the tomb of Rufus, who was brought hither in a charcoal-burner's cart from the New Forest, where the chance arrow of Tyrrel, avenged, in his last hunt, the cruelties of himself and his father on that ground. . . .

Historians claim a high antiquity for Winchester as the Cær Gwent of the Celtic and Belgic Britons, the Venta Belgarum of the Romans, and the Wintanceaster of the Saxons. The history of Winchester is nearly coeval with the Christian era. Julius Cæsar does not seem to have been here, in his invasion of Britain, but some of his troops must have passed through it; a plate from one of his standards, bearing his name and profile, having been found deep buried in a sand bed in this neighborhood; and here, within the first half century of Christendom, figured the brave descendants of Cassivelaunus, those noble sons of Cunobelin or Cymbeline, Guiderius and Arviragus, whom Shakespeare has so beautifully presented to us in his "Cymbeline." . . .

SEEING EUROPE WITH FAMOUS AUTHORS

Here it was that, while Caractacus himself reigned, the fate of the brave Queen Boadicea was sealed. Stung to the quick with the insults she had received from the Romans, this noble queen of the Iceni, the Bonduca of some writers, and the Boo Tika of her own coins, had sworn to root out the Roman power from this country. Had she succeeded, Caractacus himself had probably fallen, nor had there ever been a king Lucius here. She came, breathing utter extermination to every thing Roman or of Roman alliance, at the head of 230,000 barbarians, the most numerous army then ever collected by any British prince. Already had she visited and laid in ashes Camulodunum, London, and Verulam, killing every Roman and every Roman ally to the amount of 70,000 souls. But in this neighborhood she was met by the Roman general Paulinus, and her army routed, with the slaughter of 80,000 of her followers. In her despair at this catastrophe, she destroyed herself, and instead of entering the city in triumph was brought in, a breathless corpse, for burial.

Henry III. was born here, and always bore the name of Henry of Winchester; Henry IV. here married Joan of Brittany; Henry VI. came often hither, his first visit being to study the discipline of Wykeham's College as a model for his new one at Eton, to supply students to King's College, Cambridge, as Wykeham's does to his foundation of New College, Oxford; and happy had it been for this unfortunate monarch had he been a simple monk in one of the monasteries of a city which he so loved, enjoying peace, learning and piety, having bitterly to learn:

OTHER ENGLISH SCENES

"That all the rest is held at such a rate
As brings a thousand-fold more care to keep
Than in possession any jot of pleasure."

Henry VIII. made a visit with the Emperor Charles V., and stayed a week examining its various antiquities and religious institutions; but he afterward visited them in a more sweeping manner by the suppression of its monasteries, chantries, etc., so that, says Milner, "these being dissolved, and the edifices themselves soon after pulled down, or falling to decay, it must have worn the appearance of a city sacked by a hostile army." Through his reign and that of Edward VI., the destruction of the religious houses, and the stripping of the churches, went on to a degree which must have rendered Winchester an object of ghastly change and desolation.

"Then," says Milner, "were the precious and curious monuments of piety and antiquity, the presents of Egbert and Ethelwolph, Canute, and Emma, unrelentingly rifled and cast into the melting-pot for the mere value of the metal which composed them. Then were the golden tabernacles and images of the Apostles snatched from the cathedral and other altars," and not a few of the less valuable sort of these sacred implements were to be seen when he wrote (1798), and probably are now, in many private houses of this city and neighborhood.

The later history of this fine old city is chiefly that of melancholy and havoc. A royal marriage should be a gay thing; but the marriage of Bloody Mary here to Philip of Spain awakes no great delight in an English heart. Here, through her reign and that of Elizabeth, the chief events were persecutions for religion. James I. made Winchester the scene of the disgraceful trials of Sir Walter Raleigh, Lords Cobham and Grey, and their assumed accomplices—trials in which that most vain and pedantic of tyrants attempted, on the ground of pretended conspiracies, to wreak his personal spite on some of the best spirits of England.

VI

SCOTLAND

EDINBURGH*

BY ROBERT LOUIS STEVENSON

Venice, it has been said, differs from all other cities in the sentiment which she inspires. The rest may have admirers; she only, a famous fair one, counts lovers in her train. And, indeed, even by her kindest friends, Edinburgh is not considered in a similar sense. These like her for many reasons, not any one of which is satisfactory in itself. They like her whimsically, if you will, and somewhat as a virtuoso dotes upon his cabinet. Her attraction is romantic in the narrowest meaning of the term. Beautiful as she is, she is not so much beautiful as interesting. She is preeminently Gothic, and all the more so since she has set herself off with some Greek airs, and erected classic temples on her crags. In a word, and above all, she is a curiosity.

The palace of Holyrood has been left aside in the growth of Edinburgh, and stands gray and silent in a workman's quarter and among breweries and gas-works. It is a house of many memories. Great people of yore, kings and queens, buffoons and grave ambasadors, played their stately farce for centuries in Holyrood. Wars have been

*From "Picturesque Notes on Edinburgh."

plotted, dancing has lasted deep into the night, murder has been done in its chambers. There Prince Charlie held his fantom levées, and in a very gallant manner represented a fallen dynasty for some hours. Now, all these things of clay are mingled with the dust, the king's crown itself is shown for sixpence to the vulgar; but the stone palace has outlived these changes. For fifty weeks together, it is no more than a show for tourists and a museum of old furniture; but on the fifty-first, behold the palace reawakened and mimicking its past.

The Lord Commissioner, a kind of stage sovereign, sits among stage courtiers; a coach and six and clattering escort come and go before the gate; at night, the windows are lighted up, and its near neighbors, the workmen, may dance in their own houses to the palace music. And in this the palace is typical. There is a spark among the embers; from time to time the old volcano smokes. Edinburgh has but partly abdicated, and still wears, in parody, her metropolitan trappings. Half a capital and half a country town, the whole city leads a double existence; it has long trances of the one and flashes of the other; like the king of the Black Isles, it is half alive and half a monumental marble. There are armed men and cannon in the citadel overhead; you may see the troops marshaled on the high parade; and at night after the early winter even-fall, and in the morning before the laggard winter dawn, the wind carries abroad over Edinburgh the sound of drums and bugles. Grave judges sit bewigged in what was once the scene of imperial deliberations. Close by, in the High Street perhaps, the trumpets may sound about

SCOTLAND

the stroke of noon; and you see a troop of citizens in tawdry masquerade; tabard above, heather-mixture trouser below, and the men themselves trudging in the mud among unsympathetic bystanders. The grooms of a well-appointed circus tread the streets with a better presence. And yet these are the Heralds and Pursuivants of Scotland, who are about to proclaim a new law of the United Kingdom before two score boys, and thieves, and hackney coachmen.

Meanwhile, every hour the bell of the University rings out over the hum of the streets, and every hour a double tide of students, coming and going, fills the deep archways. And, lastly, one night in the springtime—or, say, one morning rather, at the peep of day—late folk may hear the voices of many men singing a psalm in unison from a church on one side of the Old High Street; and a little after, or perhaps a little before, the sound of many men singing a psalm in unison from another church on the opposite side of the way. There will be something in the words about the dew of Hermon, and how goodly it is to see brethren dwelling together in unity. And the late folk will tell themselves that all this singing denotes the conclusion of two yearly ecclesiastical parliaments—the parliaments of churches, which are brothers in many admirable virtues, but not specially like brothers in this particular of a tolerant and peaceful life.

Again, meditative people will find a charm in a certain consonancy between the aspect of the city and its odd and stirring history. Few places, if any, offer a more barbaric display of contrasts to the eye. In the very midst stands one of the most satisfactory crags in nature—a Bass Rock upon dry land, rooted in a garden shaken by passing trains, carrying a crown of battlements and turrets, and describing its warlike shadow over the liveliest and brightest thoroughfare of the New Town. From their smoky beehives, ten stories high, the unwashed look down upon the open squares and gardens of the wealthy; and gay people sunning themselves along Prince's Street, with its mile of commercial palaces all beflagged upon some great occasion, see, across a gardened valley set with statues, where the washings of the Old Town flutter in the breeze at its high windows.

And then, upon all sides, what a clashing of architecture! In this one valley, where the life of the town goes most busily forward, there may be seen, shown one above and behind another by the accidents of the ground, buildings in almost every style upon the globe. Egyptian and Greek temples, Venetian palaces and Gothic spires, are huddled one over another in a most admired disorder; while, above all, the brute mass of the Castle and the summit of Arthur's Seat look down upon these imitations with a becoming dignity, as the works of Nature may look down upon the monuments of Art. But Nature is a more indiscriminate patroness than we imagine, and in no way frightened of a strong effect. The birds roost as willingly among the Corinthian capitals as in the crannies of the crag; the same atmosphere and daylight clothe the eternal rock and yesterday's imitation portico; and as the soft northern sunshine throws out everything into a glorified distinctness—or easterly mists, coming up with the blue evening, fuse all these incongruous features into one, and

SCOTLAND

the lamps begin to glitter along the street, and faint lights to burn in the high windows across the valley—the feeling grows upon you that this is a piece of nature in the most intimate sense; that this profusion of eccentricities, this dream in masonry and living rock, is not a drop-scene in a theater, but a city in the world of everyday reality, connected by railway and telegraph wire with all the capitals of Europe, and inhabited by citizens of the familiar type, who keep ledgers, and attend church, and have sold their immortal portion to a daily paper. . . .

The east of new Edinburgh is guarded by a craggy hill, of no great elevation, which the town embraces. The old London road runs on one side of it; while the New Approach, leaving it on the other hand, completes the circuit. . . . Of all places for a view, this Calton Hill is perhaps the best; since you can see the Castle, which you lose from the Castle, and Arthur's Seat, which you can not see from Arthur's Seat. It is the place to stroll on one of those days of sunshine and east wind which are so common in our more than temperate summer. The breeze comes off the sea, with a little of the freshness, and that touch of chill, peculiar to the quarter, which is delightful to certain very ruddy organizations, and greatly the reverse to the majority of mankind. It brings with it a faint, floating haze, a cunning decolorizer, altho not thick enough to obscure outlines near at hand. But the haze lies more thickly to windward at the far end of Musselburgh Bay; and over the Links of Aberlady and Berwick Law and the hump of the Bass Rock it assumes the aspect of a bank of thin sea fog.

Immediately underneath, upon the south, you command the yards of the High School, and the towers and courts of the new Jail—a large place, castellated to the extent of folly, standing by itself on the edge of a steep cliff, and often joyfully hailed by tourists as the Castle. In the one, you may perhaps see female prisoners taking exercise like a string of nuns; in the other, schoolboys running at play, and their shadows keeping step with them. From the bottom of the valley, a gigantic chimney rises almost to the level of the eye, a taller and a shapelier edifice than Nelson's Monument. Look a little farther, and there is Holyrood Palace, with its Gothic frontal and ruined abbey, and the red sentry pacing smartly to and fro before the door like a mechanical figure in a panorama. By way of an outpost, you can single out the little peak-roofed lodge, over which Rizzio's murderers made their escape, and where Queen Mary herself, according to gossip, bathed in white wine to retain her loveliness.

Behind and overhead lie the Queen's Park, from Muschat's Cairn to Dumbiedykes, St. Margaret's Loch, and the long wall of Salisbury's Crags; and thence, by knoll and rocky bulwark and precipitous slope, the eye rises to the top of Arthur's Seat, a hill for magnitude, a mountain in virtue of its bold design. This upon your left. Upon the right, the roofs and spires of the Old Town climb one above another to where the citadel prints its broad bulk and jagged crown of bastions on the western sky. . . . Perhaps it is now one in the afternoon; and at the same instant of time, a ball rises to the summit of Nelson's flagstaff close at hand, and, far away, a puff of smoke, followed by a report, bursts from the half-moon battery at the Castle. This is the time-gun by which people set their watches, as far as the sea coast or in hill farms upon the Pentlands. To complete the view, the eye enfilades Prince's Street, black with traffic, and has a broad look over the valley between the Old Town and the New; here, full of railway trains and stept over by the high North Bridge upon its many columns, and there, green with trees and gardens.

On the north, the Calton Hill is neither so abrupt in itself, nor has it so exceptional an outlook; and yet even here it commands a striking prospect. A gully separates it from the New Town. This is Greenside, where witches were burned and tournaments held in former days. Down that almost precipitous bank Bothwell launched his horse, and so first, as they say, attracted the bright eyes of Mary. It is now tesselated with sheets and blankets out to dry, and the sound of people beating carpets is rarely absent. Beyond all this, the suburbs run out to Leith; Leith camps on the seaside with her forests of masts; Leith roads are full of ships at anchor; the sun picks out the white pharos upon Inchkeith Island; the Firth extends on either hand from the Ferry to the May; the towns of Fifeshire sit, each in its bank of blowing smoke, along the opposite coast; and the hills enclose the view, except to the farthest east, where the haze of the horizon rests upon the open sea. There lies the road to Norway; a dear road for Sir Patrick Spens and his Scots Lords; and yonder smoke on the hither side of Largo Law is Aberdour, from whence they sailed to seek a queen for Scotland.

These are the main features of the scene roughly

sketched. How they are all tilted by the inclination of the ground, how each stands out in delicate relief against the rest, what manifold detail, and play of sun and shadow, animate and accentuate the picture, is a matter for a person on the spot, and, turning swiftly on his heels, to grasp and bind together in one comprehensive look. It is the character of such a prospect, to be full of change and of things moving. The multiplicity embarrasses the eye; and the mind, among so much, suffers itself to grow absorbed with single points. You remark a tree in a hedgerow, or follow a cart along a country road. You turn to the city, and see children, dwarfed by distance into pigmies, at play about suburban doorsteps; you have a glimpse upon a thoroughfare where people are densely moving; you note ridge after ridge of chimney-stacks running downhill one behind another, and church spires rising bravely from the sea of roofs. At one of the innumerable windows you watch a figure moving; on one of the multitude of roofs you watch clambering chimney-sweeps. The wind takes a run and scatters the smoke; bells are heard, far and near, faint and loud, to tell the hour; or perhaps a sea bird goes dipping evenly over the housetops, like a gull across the waves. And here you are in the meantime, on this pastoral hillside, among nibbling sheep and looked upon by monumental buildings.

SCOTLAND

HOLYROOD*

BY DAVID MASSON

Mary, Queen of Scots, on her return to Scotland after her thirteen years of residence and education in France, had to form her first real acquaintance with her native shores and the capital of her realm. She had left Calais for the homeward voyage on Thursday, the 14th of August, with a retinue of about one hundred and twenty persons, French and Scottish, embarked in two French state galleys, attended by several transports. They were a goodly company, with rich and splendid baggage. The Queen's two most important uncles, indeed—the great Francis de Lorraine, Duke of Guise, and his brother, Charles de Lorraine, the Cardinal—were not on board. They, with the Duchess of Guise, and other senior lords and ladies of the French court, had bidden Mary farewell at Calais, after having accompanied her thither from Paris, and after the Cardinal had in vain tried to persuade her not to take her costly collection of pearls and other jewels with her, but to leave them in his keeping till it should be seen how she might fare among her Scottish subjects.

But on board the Queen's own galley were three others of Guise or Lorraine uncles—the Duc d'Aumale, the Grand Prior, and the Marquis d'Elbeuf—with M. Danville, son of the Constable of France, and a number of French gentlemen of lower rank, among whom one notes especially young Pierre de Bourdeilles, better known after-

*From "Edinburgh Sketches and Memories."

ward in literary history as Sieur de Brantôme, and a sprightly and poetic youth from Dauphiné, named Chastelard, one of the attendants of M. Danville. With these were mixed the Scottish contingent of the Queen's train, her four famous "Marys" included—Mary Fleming, Mary Livingstone, Mary Seton, and Mary Beaton. They had been her playfellows and little maids of honor long ago, in her Scottish childhood; they had accompanied her when she went abroad, and had lived with her ever since in France; and they were now returning with her, Scoto-French women like herself, and all of about her own age, to share her new fortunes. . . .

Then, as now, the buildings that went by the general name of Holyrood were distinguishable into two portions. There was the Abbey, now represented only by the beautiful and spacious fragment of ruin called the Royal Chapel, but then, despite the spoliations to which it had been subjected by recent English invasions, still tolerably preserved in its integrity as the famous edifice, in early Norman style, which had been founded in the twelfth century by David I., and had been enlarged in the fifteenth by additions in the later and more florid Gothic. Close by this was Holyrood House, or the Palace proper, built in the earlier part of the sixteenth century, and chiefly by James IV., to form a distinct royal dwelling, and so supersede that occasional accommodation in the Abbey itself which had sufficed for Scottish sovereigns before Edinburgh was their habitual or capital residence.

One block of this original Holyrood House still remains in the two-turreted projection of the

SCOTLAND

present Holyrood which adjoins the ruined relic of the Abbey, and which contains the rooms now specially shown as "Queen Mary's Apartments." But the present Holyrood, as a whole, is a construction of the reign of Charles II., and gives little idea of the Palace in which Mary took up her abode in 1561. The two-turreted projection on the left was not balanced then, as now, by a similar two-turreted projection on the right, with a façade of less height between, but was flanked on the right by a continued chateau-like frontage, of about the same height as the turreted projections, and at a uniform depth of recess from it, but independently garnished with towers and pinnacles. The main entrance into the Palace from the great outer courtyard was through this chateau-like flank, just about the spot where there is the entrance through the present middle façade; and this entrance led, like the present, into an inner court or quadrangle, built round on all the four sides.

That quadrangle of chateau, touching the Abbey to the back from its northeastern corner, and with the two-turreted projection to its front from its northwestern corner, constituted, indeed, the main bulk of the Palace. There were, however, extensive appurtenances of other buildings at the back or at the side farthest from the Abbey, forming minor inner courts, while part of that side of the great outer courtyard which faced the entrance was occupied by offices belonging to the Palace, and separating the courtyard from the adjacent purlieus of the town. For the grounds of both Palace and Abbey were encompassed by a wall, having gates at various points of its circuit, the principal and most strongly guarded of which was the Gothic porch admitting from the foot of the Canongate into the front courtyard. The grounds so enclosed were ample enough to contain gardens and spaces of plantation, besides the buildings and their courts. Altogether, what with the buildings themselves, what with the courts and gardens, and what with the natural grandeur of the site—a level of deep and wooded park, between the Calton heights and crags, on the one hand, and the towering shoulders of Arthur's Seat and precipitous escarpment of Salisbury Crags on the other—Holyrood in 1561 must have seemed, even to an eye the most satiated with palatial splendors abroad, a sufficiently impressive dwelling-place to be the metropolitan home of Scottish royalty.

LINLITHGOW*

BY SIR WALTER SCOTT

The convenience afforded for the sport of falconry, which was so great a favorite during the feudal ages, was probably one cause of an attachment of the ancient Scottish monarchs to Linlithgow and its fine lake. The sport of hunting was also followed with success in the neighborhood, from which circumstance it probably arises that the ancient arms of the city represent a black greyhound bitch tied to a tree. . . .

A Celt, according to Chalmers, might plausibly derive the name of Linlithgow from Lin-liah-cu, the Lake of the Greyhound. Chalmers himself seems to prefer the Gothic derivation of Linlyth-gow, or the Lake of the Great Vale. The

*From "Provincial Antiquities of Scotland."

SCOTLAND

Castle of Linlithgow is only mentioned as being a peel (a pile, that is, an embattled tower surrounded by an outwork). In 1300 it was rebuilt or repaired by Edward I., and used as one of the citadels by which he hoped to maintain his usurped dominion in Scotland. It is described by Barbour as "meihle and stark and stuffed weel." Piers Luband, a Gascoigne knight, was appointed the keeper, and appears to have remained there until the autumn of 1313, when the Scots recovered the Castle. . . .

Bruce, faithful to his usual policy, caused the peel of Linlithgow to be dismantled, and worthily rewarded William Binnock, who had behaved with such gallantry on the occasion. From this bold yeoman the Binnies of West Lothian are proud to trace their descent; and most, if not all of them, bear in their arms something connected with the wagon, which was the instrument of his stratagem.

When times of comparative peace returned, Linlithgow again became the occasional residence of the sovereign. In 1411 the town was burned by accident, and in 1414 was again subjected to the same calamity, together with the Church and Palace of the king, as is expressly mentioned by Bower. The present Church, which is a fine specimen of Gothic architecture, having a steeple surmounted by an imperial crown, was probably erected soon after the calamity.

The Palace arose from its ashes with greater splendor than before; for the family of Stuart, unhappy in some respects, were all of them fortunate in their taste for the fine arts, and particularly for that of architecture. The Lordship of

Linlithgow was settled as a dowry upon Mary of Gueldres in 1449, and again upon Margaret of Denmark in 1468.

James IV., a splendid gallant, seems to have founded the most magnificent part of Linlithgow Palace; together with the noble entrance betwixt two flanking towers bearing, on rich entablatures, the royal arms of Scotland, with the collars of the Orders of the Thistle, Garter, and Saint Michael. James IV. also erected in the Church a throne for himself, and twelve stalls for Knights Companions of the Thistle. . . . His death and the rout of his army clouded for many a day the glory of Scotland, and marred the mirth of her palaces.

James V. was much attached to Linlithgow, and added to the Palace both the Chapel and Parliament Hall, the last of which is peculiarly striking. So that when he brought his bride, Mary of Guise, there, amid the festivities which accompanied their wedding, she might have had more reason than mere complaisance for highly commending the edifice, and saying that she never saw a more princely palace. It was long her residence, and that of her royal husband, at Linlithgow. Mary was born there in an apartment still shown; and the ill-fated father, dying within a few days of that event, left the ominous diadem which he wore to the still more unfortunate infant. . . .

In the subsequent reign of Queen Mary, Linlithgow was the scene of several remarkable events; the most interesting of which was the assassination of the Regent Murray by Hamilton of Bothwellhaugh. James VI. loved the royal residence of Linlithgow, and completed the original plan of the Palace, closing the great square by a stately

SCOTLAND

range of apartments of great architectural beauty. He also made a magnificent fountain in the Palace yard, now ruinous, as are all the buildings around. Another grotesque Gothic fountain adorns the street of the town. . . .

When the scepter passed from Scotland, oblivion sat down in the halls of Linlithgow; but her absolute desolation was reserved for the memorable era of 1745-6. About the middle of January in that year, General Hawley marched at the head of a strong army to raise the siege of Stirling, then prest by the Highland insurgents under the adventurous Charles Edward. The English general had exprest considerable contempt of his enemy, who, he affirmed, would not stand a charge of cavalry. On the night of the 17th he returned to Linlithgow, with all the marks of defeat, having burned his tents, and left his artillery and baggage. His disordered troops were quartered in the Palace, and began to make such great fires on the hearth as to endanger the safety of the edifice. A lady of the Livingstone family who had apartments there remonstrated with General Hawley, who treated her fears with contempt. "I can run away from fire as fast as you can, General," answered the high-spirited dame, and with this sarcasm took horse for Edinburgh. Very soon after her departure her apprehensions were realized; the Palace of Linlithgow caught fire and was burned to the ground. The ruins alone remain to show its former splendor.

The situation of Linlithgow Palace is eminently beautiful. It stands on a promontory of some elevation, which advances almost into the midst of the lake. The form is that of a square court, composed of buildings of four stories high, with towers at the angles. The fronts within the square, and the windows, are highly ornamented, and the size of the rooms, as well as the width and character of the staircase, are upon a magnificent scale. One banquet room is 94 feet long, 30 feet wide, and 33 feet high, with a gallery for music. The king's wardrobe, or dressing-room, looking to the west, projects over the walls so as to have a delicious prospect on three sides, and is one of the most enviable boudoirs we have ever seen.

There were two main entrances to Linlithgow Palace. That from the south ascends rather steeply from the town, and passes through a striking Gothic archway, flanked by two round towers. The portal has been richly adorned by sculpture, in which can be traced the arms of Scotland with the collars of the Thistle, the Garter, and Saint Michael. This was the work of James V., and is of a most beautiful character.

The other entrance is from the eastward. The gateway is at some height from the foundation of the wall, and there are opposite to it the remains of a perron, or ramp of mason work, which those who desired to enter must have ascended by steps. A drawbridge, which could be raised at pleasure, united, when it was lowered, the ramp with the threshold of the gateway, and when raised left a gap between them, which answered the purpose of a moat. On the inside of the eastern gateway is a figure, much mutilated, said to have been that of Pope Julius II., the same Pontiff who sent to James IV. the beautiful sword which makes part of the Regalia.

SCOTLAND

"To what base offices we may return!" In the course of the last war, those beautiful remains, so full of ancient remembrances, very narrowly escaped being defaced and dishonored, by an attempt to convert them into barracks for French prisoners of war. The late President Blair, as zealous a patriot as he was an excellent lawyer, had the merit of averting this insult upon one of the most striking objects of antiquity which Scotland yet affords. I am happy to add that of late years the Court of Exchequer have, in this and similar cases, shown much zeal to preserve our national antiquities, and stop the dilapidations which were fast consuming them.

In coming to Linlithgow by the Edinburgh road, the first view of the town, with its beautiful steeple, surmounted with a royal crown, and the ruinous towers of the Palace arising out of a canopy of trees, forms a most impressive object.

STIRLING*

BY NATHANIEL HAWTHORNE

In the morning we were stirring betimes, and found Stirling to be a pretty large town, of rather ancient aspect, with many gray stone houses, the gables of which are notched on either side, like a flight of stairs. The town stands on the slope of a hill, at the summit of which, crowning a long ascent, up which the paved street reaches all the way to its gate, is Stirling Castle. Of course we

*From "English Note-Books." By special arrangement with, and by permission of, the publishers, Houghton, Mifflin Co. Copyright, 1870 and 1898.

went thither, and found free entrance, altho the castle is garrisoned by five or six hundred men, among whom are bare-legged Highlanders (I must say that this costume is very fine and becoming, tho their thighs did look blue and frost-bitten) and also some soldiers of other Scotch regiments, with tartan trousers. Almost immediately on passing the gate, we found an old artillery-man, who undertook to show us round the castle. Only a small portion of it seems to be of great antiquity. The principal edifice within the castle wall is a palace, that was either built or renewed by James VI.; and it is ornamented with strange old statues, one of which is his own.

The old Scottish Parliament House is also here. The most ancient part of the castle is the tower, where one of the Earls of Douglas was stabbed by a king, and afterward thrown out of the window. In reading this story, one imagines a lofty turret, and the dead man tumbling headlong from a great height; but, in reality, the window is not more than fifteen or twenty feet from the garden into which he fell. This part of the castle was burned last autumn; but is now under repair, and the wall of the tower is still stanch and strong. We went up into the chamber where the murder took place, and looked through the historic window.

Then we mounted the castle wall, where it broods over a precipice of many hundred feet perpendicular, looking down upon a level plain below, and forth upon a landscape, every foot of which is richly studded with historic events. There is a small peep-hole in the wall, which Queen Mary is said to have been in the habit of looking through. It is a most splendid view; in the distance, the blue Highlands, with a variety of mountain outlines that I could have studied unweariably; and in another direction, beginning almost at the foot of the Castle Hill, were the Links of Forth, where, over a plain of miles in extent the river meandered, and circled about, and returned upon itself again and again and again, as if knotted into a silver chain, which it was difficult to imagine to be all one stream. The history of Scotland might be read from this castle wall, as on a book of mighty page; for here, within the compass of a few miles, we see the field where Wallace won the battle of Stirling, and likewise the battle-field of Bannockburn, and that of Falkirk, and Sheriffmuir, and I know not how many besides.

Around the Castle Hill there is a walk, with seats for old and infirm persons, at points sheltered from the wind. We followed it downward, and I think we passed over the site where the games used to be held, and where, this morning, some of the soldiers of the garrison were going through their exercises. I ought to have mentioned, that, passing through the inner gateway of the castle, we saw the round tower, and glanced into the dungeon, where the Roderic Dhu of Scott's poem was left to die. It is one of the two round towers, between which the portcullis rose and fell.

SEEING EUROPE WITH FAMOUS AUTHORS

ABBOTSFORD*

BY WILLIAM HOWITT

Abbotsford, after twenty years' interval, and having then been seen under the doubly exaggerated influence of youth and the recent influence of Scott's poetry, in some degree disappointed me. I had imagined the house itself larger, its towers more lofty, its whole exterior more imposing. The plantations are a good deal grown, and almost bury the house from the distant view, but they still preserve all their formality of outline, as seen from the Galashiels road. Every field has a thick, black belt of fir-trees, which run about, forming on the long hillside the most fantastic figures. The house is, however, a very interesting house. At first, you come to the front next to the road, which you do by a steep descent down the plantation. You are struck, having a great castle in your imagination, with the smallness of the place. It is neither large nor lofty. Your ideal Gothic castle shrinks into a miniature. The house is quite hidden till you are at it, and then you find yourself at a small, castellated gateway, with its crosses cut into the stone pillars on each side, and the little window over it, as for the warden to look out at you.

Then comes the view of this side of the house with its portico, its bay windows with painted glass, its tall, battlemented gables, and turrets

*From "Homes and Haunts of the Most Eminent British Poets."

SCOTLAND

with their lantern terminations; the armorial escutcheon over the door, and the corbels, and then another escutcheon aloft on the wall of stars and crescents. All these have a good effect; and not less so the light screen of freestone finely worked and carved with its elliptic arches and iron lattice-work, through which the garden is seen with its espalier trees, high brick walls, and greenhouse, with a doorway at the end leading into a second garden of the same sort. The house has a dark look, being built of the native whinstone, or grau-wacke, as the Germans call it, relieved by the quoins and projections of the windows and turrets in freestone. All look classic, and not too large for the poet and antiquarian builder. The dog Maida lies in stone on the right hand of the door in the court, with the well known inscription. The house can neither be said to be Gothic nor castellated. It is a combination of the poet's, drawn from many sources, but all united by good taste, and forming an unique style, more approaching the Elizabethan than any other.

Round the court, of which the open-work screen just mentioned is the farther boundary, runs a covered walk, that is, along the two sides not occupied by the house and the screen; and in the wall beneath the arcade thus formed, are numerous niches, containing a medley of old figures brought from various places. There are Indian gods, old figures out of churches, and heads of Roman emperors. In the corner of the court, on the opposite side of the portico to the dog Maida, is a fountain, with some similar relics reared on the stone-work around it.

SEEING EUROPE WITH FAMOUS AUTHORS

The other front gives you a much greater idea of the size. It has a more continuous range of façade. Here, at one end, is Scott's square tower, ascended by outside steps, and a round or octagon tower at the other; you can not tell, certainly, which shape it is, as it is covered with ivy. On this the flag-staff stands. At the end next to the square tower, i. e., at the right-hand end as you face it, you pass into the outer court, which allows you to go around the end of the house from one front to the other, by the old gate-way, which once belonged to the Tolbooth of Edinburgh. Along the whole of this front runs a gallery, in which the piper used to stalk to and fro while they were at dinner. This man still comes about the place, tho he has been long discharged. He is a great vagabond.

Such is the exterior of Abbotsford. The interior is far more interesting. The porch, copied from that of the old palace of Linlithgow, is finely groined, and there are stags' horns nailed up in it. When the door opens, you find yourself in the entrance-hall, which is, in fact, a complete museum of antiquities and other matters. It is, as described in Lockhart's Life of Scott, wainscoted with old wainscot from the kirk of Dumfermline, and the pulpit of John Knox is cut in two, and placed as chiffoniers between the windows. The whole walls are covered with suits of armor and arms, horns of moose deer, the head of a musk bull, etc. At your left hand, and close to the door, are two cuirasses, some standards, eagles, etc., collected at Waterloo.

At the opposite end of the room are two full suits of armor, one Italian, and one English of

SCOTLAND

the time of Henry V., the latter holding in its hands a stupendous two-handed sword, I suppose six feet long, and said to have been found on Bosworth field. Opposite to the door is the fireplace of freestone, imitated from an arch in the cloister at Melrose, with a peculiarly graceful spandrel. In it stands the iron grate of Archbishop Sharpe, who was murdered by the Covenanters; and before it stands a most massive Roman camp-kettle. On the roof, at the center of the pointed arches, runs a row of escutcheons of Scott's family, two or three at one end being empty, the poet not being able to trace the maternal lineage so high as the paternal. These were painted accordingly in clouds, with the motto, "Night veils the deep." Around the door at one end are emblazoned the shields of his most intimate friends, as Erskine, Moritt, Rose, etc., and all around the cornice ran the emblazoned shields of the old chieftains of the border. . . .

Then there is the library, a noble room, with a fine cedar ceiling, with beautiful compartments, and most lovely carved pendants, where you see bunches of grapes, human figures, leaves, etc. It is copied from Rosslyn or Melrose. There are three busts in this room; the first, one of Sir Walter, by Chantrey; one of Wordsworth; and in the great bay window, on a table, a cast of that of Shakespeare, from Stratford. There is a full-length painting of the poet's son, the present Sir Walter, in his hussar uniform, with his horse. The work-table in the space of the bay window, and the fine carved ceiling in this part of the room, as well as the brass hanging lamp brought from Herculaneum, are particularly worthy of notice. There is a pair of most splendidly carved box-wood chairs, brought from Italy, and once belonging to some cardinal. The other chairs are of ebony, presented by George IV. There is a tall silver urn, standing on a prophyry table, filled with bones from the Piræus, and inscribed as the gift of Lord Byron. The books in this room, many of which are secured from hurt by wire-work doors are said to amount to twenty thousand. Many, of course, are very valuable, having been collected with great care by Scott, for the purpose of enabling him to write his different works. . . .

The armory is a most remarkable room; it is the collection of the author of Waverly; and to enumerate all the articles which are here assembled, would require a volume. Take a few particulars. The old wooden lock of the Tolbooth of Selkirk; Queen Mary's offering-box, a small iron ark or coffer, with a circular lid, found in Holyrood-house. Then Hofer's rifle—a short, stout gun, given him by Sir Humphry Davy, or rather by Hofer's widow to Sir Humphry for Sir Walter. The housekeeper said, that Sir Humphry had done some service for the widow of Hofer, and in her gratitude she offered him this precious relic, which he accepted for Sir Walter, and delighted the poor woman with the certainty that it would be preserved to posterity in such a place as Abbotsford. There is an old white hat, worn by the burgesses of Stowe when installed. Rob Roy's purse and his gun; a very long one, with the initials R. M. C., Robert Macgregor Campbell, around the touch-hole. A rich sword in a silver sheath, presented to Sir Walter

SCOTLAND

by the people of Edinburgh, for the pains he took when George IV. was there. . . .

Lastly, and on our way back to the entrance-hall, we enter the writing-room of Sir Walter, which is surrounded by book-shelves, and a gallery, by which Scott not only could get at his books, but by which he could get to and from his bedroom; and so be at work when his visitors thought him in bed. He had only to lock his door, and he was safe. Here are his easy leathern chair and desk, at which he used to work, and, in a little closet, is the last suit that he ever wore—a bottle-green coat, plaid waistcoat, of small pattern, gray plaid trousers, and white hat. Near these hang his walking-stick, and his boots and walking-shoes. Here are, also, his tools, with which he used to prune his trees in the plantations, and his yeoman-cavalry accoutrements. On the chimney-piece stands a German light-machine, where he used to get a light, and light his own fire. There is a chair made of the wood of the house at Robroyston, in which William Wallace was betrayed; having a brass plate in the back, stating that it is from this house, where "Wallace was done to death by Traitors." The writing-room is connected with the library, and this little closet had a door issuing into the garden; so that Scott had all his books at immediate command, and could not only work early and late, without anybody's knowledge, but, at will, slip away to wood and field, if he pleased, unobserved.

DRYBURGH ABBEY*

BY WILLIAM HOWITT

Dryburgh lies amid the scenes in which Scott not only took such peculiar delight, but which furnished him themes both for his poems and romances, and which were rich in those old songs and narratives of border feats and raids which he has preserved in his Border Minstrelsy. Melrose, the Eildon Hills, the haunt of Thomas of Ercildoune, Jedburgh, Yetholm, the Cowdenknowes, the Yarrow, and Ettrick, all lie on different sides within a circle of twenty miles, and most of them much nearer. Smailholme Tower, the scene of some of Scott's youthful days, and of his ballad of "The Eve of St. John," is also one of these. Grose tells us that "The ruins of Dryburgh Monastery are beautifully situated on a peninsula formed by the Tweed, ten-miles above Kelso, and three below Melrose, on the southwestern confine of the county of Berwick." . . .

The new Abbey of Dryburgh had the credit of being founded in 1150 by David I., who was fond of the reputation of being a founder of abbeys, Holyrood Abbey, Melrose Abbey, Kelso Abbey, Jedburgh Abbey, and others, having David I. stated as their founder. However it might be in other cases, and in some of them he was merely the restorer, the real founders of Dryburgh were Hugh de Morville, Lord of Lauderdale, and Constable of Scotland, and his wife, Beatrice de Beauchamp. . . .

*From "The Ruined Abbeys of the Border."

SCOTLAND

Edward II., in his invasion of Scotland in 1323, burned down Dryburgh Abbey, as he had done that of Melrose in the preceding year; and both these magnificent houses were restored principally at the cost of Robert Bruce. It was again destroyed by the English in 1544, by Sir George Bowes and Sir Brian Latoum, as Melrose was also. Among the most distinguished of its abbots we may mention Andrew Fordum, Bishop of Moray, and afterward Archbishop of St. Andrews, and Ambassador to France, and who held some of the most important offices under James IV. and James V. The favors conferred upon him were in proportion to his consequence in the state. Along with this abbey of Dryburgh, he held in commendam those of Pittenweem, Coldingham, and Dunfermline. He resigned Dryburgh to James Ogilvie, of the family of Deskford. Ogilvie was also considerably employed in offices of diplomacy, both at London and Paris.

The Erskines seemed to keep firm hold of the Abbey of Dryburgh; and Adam Erskine, one of Abbot James's successors, was, under George Buchanan, a sub-preceptor to James VI. This James I. of England dissolved the abbey in 1604, and conferred it and its lands, together with the abbeys and estates of Cambuskenneth and Inchmahorne, on John Erskine, Earl of Mar, who was made, on this occasion, also Baron of Cardross, which barony was composed of the property of these three monasteries. In this line, Dryburgh descended to the Lords of Buchan. The Earls of Buchan, at one time, sold it to the Halliburtons of Mortoun, from whom it was purchased by Colonel Tod, whose heirs again sold it to the Earl of Buchan in 1786. This eccentric nobleman bequeathed it to his son, Sir David Erskine, at whose death in 1837 it reverted to the Buchan family.

Two monasteries in Ireland, the abbey of Druin-la-Croix in the County of Armagh, and the abbey of Woodburn in the county of Antrim, acknowledged Dryburgh as their mother. A copy of the Liber S. Mariæ de Dryburgh is in the Advocates' Library in Edinburgh, containing all its ancient charters. Such are the main points of history connected with Dryburgh; but, when we open the ballad lore of the South of Scotland, we find this fine old place figuring repeatedly and prominently. . . .

Grose says: "The freestone of which the monastery of Dryburgh and the most elegant parts of the Abbey of Melrose were built, is one of a most beautiful color and texture, and has defied the influence of the weather for more than six centuries; nor is the sharpness of the sculpture in the least affected by the ravages of time. The quarry from which it was taken is still successfully worked at Dryburgh; and no stone in the island seems more perfectly adapted for the purpose of architecture, as it hardens by age, and is not subject to be corroded or decomposed by the weather, so that it might even be used for the cutting of bas-reliefs and of statues." . . .

As the remains of the abbey have since been carefully preserved, they present still much the same aspect as at Grose's visit in 1797. When I visited this lovely ruin and lovely neighborhood in 1845, I walked from Melrose, a distance of between three and four miles. Leaving the Eildon Hills on my right, and following the course of the Tweed, I saw, as I progressed, Cowdenknowes, Bemerside, and other spots famous in border song. Issuing from a steep and woody lane, I came out on a broad bend of the river, with a wide strand of gravel and stones on this side, showing with what force the wintry torrents rushed along here. Opposite rose lofty and finely-wooded banks. Amid the trees on that side shone out a little temple of the Muses, where they are represented as consecrating James Thomson the poet. Farther off, on a hill, stands a gigantic statue of William Wallace, which was orginally intended for Burns; but, the stone being too large, it was thought by the eccentric Lord Buchan, who erected it, a pity to cut it down.

. . .

I was ferried over by two women, who were by no means sorry that the winds and floods had carried my Lord Buchan's bridge away, as it restored their business of putting people over. I then ascended a lane from the ferry, and found myself in front of an apparently old castle gateway; but, from the Latin inscription over it, discovered that it was also erected by the same singular Lord Buchan, as the entrance to a pomarium, or, in plain English, an orchard, dedicated to his honored parents, who, I suppose, like our first parents, were particularly fond of apples. That his parents or himself might enjoy all the apples, he had under the Latin dedication, placed a simple English menace of steel traps and spring guns. I still advanced through a pleasant scene of trees and cottages, of rich grassy crofts, with cattle lying luxuriously in them, and amid a hush of repose, indicative of a monastic scene.

Having found a guide to the ruins, at a cottage near the river, I was led across a young orchard toward them, the two old gables and the fine circular window showing themselves above the foliage. I found the interior of the ruins carpeted by soft turf, and two rows of cedars growing in the church, marking where the aisle formerly ran. The cloisters and south transept were still entire, and displayed much fine workmanship. The great circular window is especially lovely, formed of five stars cut in stone, so that the open center between them forms a rose. The light seen through this charming window produced a fine effect. The chapter-house was also entire, the floor being now only of earth; and a circle was drawn in the center, where the remains of the founder and his lady lie. Here, again, however, the fantastic old Lord Buchan had interfered, and a statue of Locke, reading an open book, and pointing to his own forehead; one of Inigo Jones, and one of Newton, made you wonder what they were doing there. So totally without regard to fitness did this half-crazy nobleman put down his ornaments. The wonder is that his successor had not removed these, and some statues or busts which had as little business on the spot.

But the charm of the place in every sense was the grave of Scott. It was in the Lady aisle, and occupies two arches of it; and the adjoining space under the next arch is the burial place of the Erskines, as Scott's burial-place was that of

Copyright by Underwood & Underwood, N. Y.

STIRLING CASTLE

RUINS OF HOLYROOD ABBEY, EDINBURGH

MELROSE ABBEY

GLASTONBURY ABBEY
(See Vol. I for an account of Glastonbury)

CRAIGMILLAR CASTLE, SCOTLAND

DUMBARTON ROCK AND CASTLE FROM THE RIVER CLYDE

LIMERICK CASTLE

ST. PATRICK'S CATHEDRAL, DUBLIN

THE GIANT'S CAUSEWAY

BLARNEY CASTLE

MUCROSS ABBEY

THE LAKES OF KILLARNEY

SACKVILLE STREET, DUBLIN

THE GAP OF DUNLOE

SCOTLAND

his ancestors, the Halliburtons. The whole, with the tier of small sectional Norman arches above, forms a glorious tomb much resembling one of the chapel tombs in Winchester Cathedral. Taken in connection with the fine ruins, and the finer natural scenery around, no spot can be supposed more suitable for the resting-place of the remains of the great minstrel and romancer, who so delighted in the natural, historic, and legendary charms of the neighborhood, and who added still greater ones to them himself.

Since my visit, a massive tomb, of Aberdeen granite, has been placed over the remains of Sir Walter and Lady Scott, and those of their eldest son. A railway also now makes the place much more accessible, the station for Drybrugh being at the village of Newtown, on the other side of the river. Near St. Boswell's, opposite to Dryburgh, has also been lately erected a bridge over the Tweed, opening up the communication betwixt the north and south side of the river, and thus enabling the tourist to explore at great convenience the scenes of ancient loves and feuds, and the haunts of Scott. Here his dust lies amid the objects redolent of his fame; and within a few miles, near Makerstoun, a view may be obtained, from a hill, of Smailholme Tower, where the poet passed some of the years of his boyhood, and the memory of which he has perpetuated in one of the epistles which introduce each Canto of Marmion.

MELROSE ABBEY*

BY WILLIAM HOWITT.

The foundation of Melrose Abbey generally dates from 1136, when David I. of Scotland, among his many similar erections, built a church here. But Melrose, as a seat of religion, boasts a much earlier origin. It was one of those churches, or more properly missionary stations, which the fathers of Ireland and of Iona spread over Britain and the continent. It was in fact a portion of that pure and beautiful British church which existed prior to the Roman hierarchy in these islands, and of which the professors presented in their primitive habits and primitive doctrines so apostolic a character. . . .

In 1136 the pious David raised a new and much superior abbey, about two miles westward of the original site, but on the same south bank of the Tweed, and established in it the Cistercians. He conferred on them extensive lands and privileges; the lands of Melrose, Eldun, and Dernwie; the lands and wood of Gattonside, with the fishings of the Tweed along the whole extent of those lands; with the right of pasturage and pannage in his forests of Selkirk and Traguair, and in the forest between the Gala and the Leeder, with wood from those forests for building and burning. In 1192 Jocelin, Bishop of Glasgow, granted to the monks of Melrose the church of Hassindean, with its lands, tithes, and other emoluments, "for the maintenance of the poor and of pilgrims coming to the

*From "The Ruined Abbeys of the Border."

house of Melrose." From this cause the old tower of Hassindean was called "Monks' Tower," and the farm adjoining the church is still called "Monks' Croft." In fact, the Abbey of Melrose was a sort of inn, not only to the poor, but to some of the greatest men of the time. The Scottish kings from time to time, and wealthy subjects too, added fresh grants; so that in the twelfth and thirteenth centuries the Abbey had accumulated vast possessions and immunities; had many tenants, great husbandmen, with many granges and numerous herds. It had much other property in Ayrshire, Dumfriesshire, Selkirkshire, and Berwickshire.

But the abbey church which David built was not that of which we have now the remains. The whole place was repeatedly burned down by the English invaders. In 1215 the rebellious barons of King John of England swore fealty to Alexander II. of Scotland, at the altar of Melrose. Edward I., in 1295-6, when at Berwick, granted the monks of Melrose restitution of the lands of which they had been deprived; but in 1332 Edward II. burned down the abbey and killed the abbot William de Peeblis and several of his monks. Robert I., of Scotland. in 1326 or four years afterward, gave £2,000 sterling to rebuild it; and Edward II., of England, came from New Castle at Christmas, 1341, and held his yule in the abbey, and made restitution of the lands and other property which his father had seized during the late war. In 1378 Richard II. granted a protection to the abbot and his lands; but in 1385 he burned down Melrose and other religious houses on his expedition into Scotland.

Robert Bruce, in the beginning of the fourteenth century, granted a revenue to restore the abbey; and betwixt this period and the Reformation arose the splendid structure, the ruins of which yet charm every eye. It is in the highest style of the decorated order, every portion is full of work of the most exquisite character, occasionally mingled with the perpendicular. They are the only ruins of the church which remain, and they present the finest specimen of Gothic architecture and sculpture that Scotland possesses. One of Scotland's most discriminating writers says, "To say that Melrose is beautiful, is to say nothing. It is exquisitely—splendidly lovely. It is an object possest of infinite grace and unmeasurable charm; it is fine in its general aspect, and in its minutest details. It is a study—a glory." The church is two hundred and eighty-seven feet in length, and at the greatest breadth one hundred and fifty-seven feet. The west is wholly ruined; but the great eastern window remains, and one above the southern door, which are extremely fine. The pillars that remain to support the roof are of singular grace, and wherever you turn you behold objects that rivet the attention by their richness of sculpture, tho often only in fragments. The only wonder is that so much has escaped the numberless assaults of enemies.

During the reigns of Henry VIII., Edward VI., and Elizabeth, the abbey was continually suffering from their inroads, in which the spirit of vengeance against the Scots who resisted their schemes of aggression was mixed strongly with that of enmity to Popery. In the year 1545, it was twice burned and ransacked by the Eng-

SCOTLAND

lish, first under Sir Ralph Eyre and Sir Bryan Layton, and again by the Earl of Hertford. At the Reformation, when all its lands and immunities were invested in the Crown, they were valued at £1,758 Scots, besides large contributions in kind. Among them, in addition to much corn were one hundred and five stones of butter, ten dozens of capons, twenty-six dozens of poultry, three hundred and seventy-six more fowl, three hundred and forty loads of peats, etc. Queen Mary granted Melrose and its lands and tithes to Bothwell, but they were forfeited on his attainder. They then passed to a Douglas, and afterward to Sir James Ramsay, who rescued James VI. in the conspiracy of Gowrie; then to Sir Thomas Hamilton in 1619, who was made Earl of Melrose, and afterward Earl of Haddington.

About a century ago they became the property of the family of Buccleuch, in which they remain. The Douglas built himself a house out of the ruins, which may still be seen about fifty yards to the north of the church. The ruins are preserved with great care, and are shown by a family which is at once intelligent and courteous. The person going round, most generally, points out the shattered remains of thirteen figures at the great eastern window, in their niches, said to have been those of our Savior and his Apostles. They were broken to pieces by a fanatic weaver of Gattonside. A head is also pointed out, said to be that of Michael Scott, the magician, who exerted his power so wonderfully, according to tradition, in this neighborhood, as to split the Eildon hill into three parts. . . .

The name of Melrose is clearly derived from

the Ancient British, Melross, the projection of the meadow. Moel in Welsh and Maol in Irish signify something bald, naked, bare. Thus Moal-Ross, in the language of the Irish monks who first built the church here, would signify the naked promontory. Moel in Welsh is now usually applied to a smooth mountain, as Moel-Siabod; and we find Ross continually showing its Celtic origin where there is a promontory, as Ross on the Moray-frith, and Ross in Herefordshire from a winding of the Wye. But some old sculptor, on a stone still preserved in the village, has made a punning derivation for it, by carving a mell, or mallet, and a rose over it. This stone was part of a wall of the old prison, long since pulled down.

The site of Melrose, like all monastic ones, is fine. The abbey stands on a broad level near the Tweed, but is surrounded by hills and fields full of beauty, and peopled with a thousand beings of romance, tradition, and poetry. South of the village rise the three peaks of the Eildon hill, bearing aloft the fame of Michael Scott and Thomas the Rhymer. On the banks of the Tweed, opposite to Melrose, lies Gattonside, buried in its gardens and orchards, and still retaining its faith in many a story of the supernatural; and about three miles westward, on the same bank of the river, stands Abbotsford, raised by a magician more mighty than Michael Scott. How is it possible to approach that haunted abode without meeting on the way the most wonderful troop of wild, and lofty, and beautiful beings that ever peopled earth or the realm of imagination? Scotch, English, Gallic, Indian, Syrian come forth to meet you. The Bruce, the Scottish Jameses, Coeur de

SCOTLAND

Lion, Elizabeth, Leicester, Mary of Scots, James I. of England, Montrose, Claverhouse, Cumberland the Butcher. The Covenanters are ready to preach and fight anew, the Highland clans rise in aid of the Stuart. What women of dazzling beauty—Flora M'Ivor, Rose Bradwardine, Rebecca the noble Jewess, Lucy Ashton, and Amy Robsart, the lovely Effie Deans, and her homely yet glorious sister Jenny, the bewitching Di Vernon, and Minna and Brenda Troil, of the northern isles, stand radiant amid a host of lesser beauties.

Then comes Rob Roy, the Robin Hood of the hills; then Balfour of Burley issues, a stalwart apparition, from his hiding-place, and of infinite humor and strangeness of aspect. Where' is there a band like this—the Baron of Bradwardine, Dominie Sampson, Meg Merrilies, Monkbarns, Edie Ochiltree, Old Mortality, Bailie Nicol Jarvie, Andrew Fairservice, Caleb Balderston, Flibbertigibbet, Mona of the Fitful head, and that fine fellow the farmer of Liddesdale, with all his Peppers and Mustards raffling at his heels? But not even out of Melrose need you move a step to find the name of a faithful servant of Sir Walter. Tom Purdie lies in Melrose Abbey-Yard; and Scott himself had engraven on his tomb that he was "the Wood-forester of Abbotsford," probably the title which Tom gave himself. Those who visit Melrose will take a peep at the gravestone of Tom Purdie, who sleeps amid a long line of the dead, reaching from the days of Aidan to our own, as alive he filled a little niche in the regard of a master who has given to both high and low so many niches in the temple of immortality.

CARLYLE'S BIRTHPLACE AND EARLY HOMES*

BY JOHN BURROUGHS.

There was no road in Scotland or England which I should have been so glad to have walked over as that from Edinburgh to Ecclefechan, a distance covered many times by the feet of him whose birth and burial place I was about to visit. Carlyle as a young man had walked it with Edward Irving (the Scotch say "travel" when they mean going afoot), and he had walked it alone, and as a lad with an elder boy, on his way to Edinburgh College. He says in his "Reminiscences" he nowhere else had such affectionate, sad, thoughtful, and in fact interesting and salutary journeys. . . .

Not to be entirely cheated out of my walk, I left the train at Lockerby, a small Scotch market-town, and accomplished the remainder of the journey to Ecclefechan on foot, a brief six-mile pull. It was the first day of June; the afternoon sun was shining brightly. It was still the honeymoon of travel with me, not yet two weeks in the bonnie land; the road was smooth and clean as the floor of a sea beach, and firmer, and my feet devoured the distance with right good will. . . .

Four miles from Lockerby I came to Mainhill, the name of a farm where the Carlyle family lived many years, and where Carlyle first read Goethe, "in a dry ditch," Froude says, and translated

*From "Fresh Fields." By special arrangement with, and by permission of, the publishers, Houghton, Mifflin Co. Copyright, 1884.

SCOTLAND

"Wilhelm Meister." The land drops gently away to the south and east, opening up broad views in these directions, but it does not seem to be the bleak and windy place Froude describes it. The crops looked good, and the fields smooth and fertile. The soil is rather a stubborn clay, nearly the same as one sees everywhere. . . .

The Carlyles were living on this farm while their son was teaching school at Annan, and later at Kircaldy with Irving, and they supplied him with cheese, butter, ham, oatmeal, etc., from their scanty stores. A new farm-house has been built since then, tho the old one is still standing; doubtless the same Carlyle's father refers to in a letter to his son, in 1817, as being under way. The parish minister was expected at Mainhill. "Your mother was very anxious to have the house done before he came, or else she said she would run over the hill and hide herself."

From Mainhill the highway descends slowly to the village of Ecclefechan, the site of which is marked to the eye, a mile or more away, by the spire of the church rising up against a background of Scotch firs, which clothe a hill beyond. I soon enter the main street of the village, which in Carlyle's youth had an open burn or creek flowing through the center of it. This has been covered over by some enterprising citizen, and instead of a loitering little burn, crossed by numerous bridges, the eye is now greeted by a broad expanse of small cobble-stones. The cottages are for the most part very humble, and rise from the outer edges of the pavement, as if the latter had been turned up and shaped to make their walls. The church is a handsome brown-stone structure, of recent date, and is more in keeping with the fine fertile country about than with the little village in its front. In the cemetery back of it, Carlyle lies buried. As I approached, a girl sat by the road-side, near the gate, combing her black locks and arranging her toilet; waiting, as it proved, for her mother and brother, who lingered in the village. A couple of boys were cutting nettles against the hedge; for the pigs, they said, after the sting had been taken out of them by boiling. Across the street from the cemetery the cows of the villagers were grazing.

I must have thought it would be as easy to distinguish Carlyle's grave from the others as it was to distinguish the man while living, or his fame when dead; for it never occurred to me to ask in what part of the inclosure it was placed. Hence, when I found myself inside the gate, which opens from the Annan road through a high stone wall, I followed the most worn path toward a new and imposing-looking monument on the far side of the cemetery; and the edge of my fine emotion was a good deal dulled against the marble when I found it bore a strange name. I tried others, and still others, but was disappointed. I found a long row of Carlyles, but he whom I sought was not among them. My pilgrim enthusiasm felt itself needlessly hindered and chilled. How many rebuffs could one stand? Carlyle dead, then, was the same as Carlyle living; sure to take you down a peg or two when you came to lay your homage at his feet.

Presently I saw "Thomas Carlyle" on a big marble slab that stood in a family inclosure. But this turned out to be the name of a nephew of the

SCOTLAND

great Thomas. However, I had struck the right plat at last; here were the Carlyles I was looking for, within a space probably of eight by sixteen feet, surrounded by a high iron fence. The latest made grave was higher and fuller than the rest, but it had no stone or mark of any kind to distinguish it. Since my visit, I believe, a stone or monument of some kind has been put up. A few daisies and the pretty blue-eyed speedwell were growing amid the grass upon it. The great man lies with his head toward the south or southwest, with his mother, sister, and father to the right of him, and his brother John to the left. I was glad to learn that the high iron fence was not his own suggestion. His father had put it around the family plot in his lifetime. Carlyle would have liked to have it cut down about half-way. The whole look of the cemetery, except in the size of the head-stones, was quite American. . . .

A young man and his wife were working in a nursery of young trees, a few paces from the graves and I conversed with them through a thin place in the hedge. They said they had seen Carlyle many times, and seemed to hold him in proper esteem and reverence. The young man had seen him come in summer and stand, with uncovered head, beside the graves of his father and mother. "And long and reverently did he remain there, too," said the young gardener. I learned this was Carlyle's invariable custom: every summer did he make a pilgrimage to this spot, and with bared head linger beside these graves. The last time he came, which was a couple of years before he died, he was so feeble that two persons sustained him while he walked into the cemetery.

BURNS'S LAND*

BY NATHANIEL HAWTHORNE.

We left Carlisle at a little past eleven, and within the half-hour were at Gretna Green. Thence we rushed onward into Scotland through a flat and dreary tract of country, consisting mainly of desert and bog, where probably the moss-troopers were accustomed to take refuge after their raids into England. Anon, however, the hills hove themselves up to view, occasionally attaining a height which might almost be called mountainous. In about two hours we reached Dumfries, and alighted at the station there. . . .

We asked for Burns's dwelling; and a woman pointed across a street to a two-story house, built of stone, and whitewashed, like its neighbors, but perhaps of a little more respectable aspect than most of them, tho I hesitate in saying so. It was not a separate structure, but under the same continuous roof with the next. There was an inscription on the door, bearing no reference to Burns, but indicating that the house was now occupied by a ragged or industrial school. On knocking, we were instantly admitted by a servant-girl, who smiled intelligently when we told our errand, and showed us into a low and very plain parlor, not more than twelve or fifteen feet square. A young woman, who seemed to be a teacher in the school, soon appeared, and told us that this had been Burns's usual sitting-room, and that he had written many of his songs here.

*From "Our Old Home." Published by Houghton, Mifflin Co.

SCOTLAND

She then led us up a narrow staircase into a little bed-chamber over the parlor. Connecting with it, there is a very small room, or windowed closet, which Burns used as a study; and the bed-chamber itself was the one where he slept in his later lifetime, and in which he died at last. Altogether, it is an exceedingly unsuitable place for a pastoral and rural poet to live or die in,—even more unsatisfactory than Shakespeare's house, which has a certain homely picturesqueness that contrasts favorably with the suburban sordidness of the abode before us. . . .

Coming to St. Michael's Church, we saw a man digging a grave, and, scrambling out of the hole, he let us into the churchyard, which was crowded full of monuments. There was a footpath through this crowded churchyard, sufficiently well worn to guide us to the grave of Burns, but a woman followed behind us, who, it appeared, kept the key to the mausoleum, and was privileged to show it to strangers. The monument is a sort of Grecian temple, with pilasters and a dome, covering a space of about twenty feet square. It was formerly open to all the inclemencies of the Scotch atmosphere, but is now protected and shut in by large squares of rough glass, each pane being of the size of one whole side of the structure. The woman unlocked the door, and admitted us into the interior. Inlaid into the floor of the mausoleum is the gravestone of Burns—the very same that was laid over his grave by Jean Armour, before this monument was built. Displayed against the surrounding wall is a marble statue of Burns at the plow, with the Genius of Caledonia summoning the

109

plowman to turn poet. Methought it was not a very successful piece of work; for the plow was better sculptured than the man, and the man, tho heavy and cloddish, was more effective than the goddess. Our guide informed us that an old man of ninety, who knew Burns, certifies this statue to be very like the original.

The bones of the poet, and of Jean Armour, and of some of their children, lie in the vault over which we stood. Our guide (who was intelligent, in her own plain way, and very agreeable to talk withal) said that the vault was opened about three weeks ago, on occasion of the burial of the eldest son of Burns.* The poet's bones were disturbed, and the dry skull, once so brimming over with powerful thought and bright and tender fantasies, was taken away and kept for several days by a Dumfries doctor. It has since been deposited in a new leaden coffin, and restored to the vault.

We went into the church, and found it very plain and naked, without altar-decorations, and having its floor quite covered with unsightly wooden pews. The woman led us to a pew cornering on one of the side-aisles, and, telling us that it used to be Burns's family pew, showed us his seat, which is in the corner by the aisle. It is so situated, that a sturdy pillar hid him from the pulpit, and from the minister's eye; "for Robin was no great friends with the ministers," said she. This touch—his seat behind the pillar, and Burns himself nodding in sermon time, or keenly observant of profane things—brought him before

*This was written in 1860.

us to the life. In the corner-seat of the next pew, right before Burns, and not more than two feet off, sat the young lady on whom the poet saw that unmentionable parasite which he has immortalized in song. We were ungenerous enough to ask the lady's name, but the good woman could not tell it. This was the last thing which we saw in Dumfries worthy of record; and it ought to be noted that our guide refused some money which my companion offered her, because I had already paid her what she deemed sufficient.

At the railway station we spent more than a weary hour, waiting for the train, which at last came up, and took us to Mauchline. We got into an omnibus, the only conveyance to be had, and drove about a mile to the village, where we established ourselves at the Loudoun Hotel, one of the veriest country inns which we have found in Great Britain. The town of Mauchline, a place more redolent of Burns than almost any other, consists of a street or two of contiguous cottages, mostly whitewashed, and with thatched roofs. It has nothing sylvan or rural in the immediate village, and is as ugly a place as mortal man could contrive to make, or to render uglier through a succession of untidy generations. The fashion of paving the village street, and patching one shabby house on the gable-end of another, quite shuts out all verdure and pleasantness; but, I presume, we are not likely to see a more genuine old Scotch village, such as they used to be in Burns's time, and long before, than this of Mauchline. The church stands about midway up the street, and is built of red freestone, very simple in its architecture, with a square tower and pinnacles. In this sacred edifice, and its churchyard, was the scene of one of Burns's most characteristic productions, "The Holy Fair."

Almost directly opposite its gate, across the village street, stands Posie Nansie's inn, where the "Jolly Beggars" congregated. The latter is a two-story, red-stone, thatched house, looking old, but by no means venerable, like a drunken patriarch. It has small, old-fashioned windows, and may well have stood for centuries—tho seventy or eighty years ago, when Burns was conversant with it, I should fancy it might have been something better than a beggar's alehouse. . . .

[Burns's farm of] Moss Giel is not more than a mile from Mauchline, and the road extends over a high ridge of land, with a view of far hills and green slopes on either side. Just before we reached the farm, the driver stopt to point out a hawthorn, growing by the wayside, which he said was Burns's "Lousie Thorn"; and I devoutly plucked a branch, altho I have really forgotten where or how this illustrious shrub has been celebrated. We then turned into a rude gateway, and almost immediately came to the farm-house of Moss Giel, standing some fifty yards removed from the high-road, behind a tall hedge of hawthorn, and considerably overshadowed by trees.

The biographers talk of the farm of Moss Giel as being damp and unwholesome; but I do not see why, outside of the cottage walls, it should possess so evil a reputation. It occupies a high, broad ridge, enjoying, surely, whatever benefit can come of a breezy site, and sloping far downward before any marshy soil is reached. The high hedge, and the trees that stand beside the cottage,

SCOTLAND

give it a pleasant aspect enough to one who does not know the grimy secrets of the interior; and the summer afternoon was now so bright that I shall remember the scene with a great deal of sunshine over it.

Leaving the cottage, we drove through a field, which the driver told us was that in which Burns turned up the mouse's nest. It is the enclosure nearest to the cottage, and seems now to be a pasture, and a rather remarkably unfertile one. A little farther on, the ground was whitened with an immense number of daisies—daisies, daisies everywhere; and in answer to my inquiry, the driver said that this was the field where Burns ran his plowshare over the daisy. If so, the soil seems to have been consecrated to daisies by the song which he bestowed on that first immortal one. I alighted, and plucked a whole handful of these "wee, modest, crimson-tipped flowers," which will be precious to many friends in our own country as coming from Burns's farm, and being of the same race and lineage as that daisy which he turned into an amaranthine flower while seeming to destroy it. From Moss Giel we drove through a variety of pleasant scenes, some of which were familiar to us by their connection with Burns.

By and by we came to the spot where Burns saw Miss Alexander, the Lass of Ballochmyle. It was on a bridge, which (or, more probably, a bridge that has succeeded to the old one, and is made of iron) crosses from bank to bank, high in air, over a deep gorge of the road; so that the young lady may have appeared to Burns like a creature between earth and sky, and compounded chiefly of celestial elements. But, in honest truth, the great charm of a woman, in Burns's eyes, was always her womanhood, and not the angelic mixture which other poets find in her.

Our driver pointed out the course taken by the Lass of Ballochmyle, through the shrubbery, to a rock on the banks of the Lugar, where it seems to be the tradition that Burns accosted her. The song implies no such interview. Lovers, of whatever condition, high or low, could desire no lovelier scene in which to breathe their vows: the river flowing over its pebbly bed, sometimes gleaming into the sunshine, sometimes hidden deep in verdure, and here and there eddying at the foot of high and precipitous cliffs.

Our ride to Ayr presented nothing very remarkable; and, indeed, a cloudy and rainy day takes the varnish off the scenery and causes a woful diminution in the beauty and impressiveness of everything we see. Much of our way lay along a flat, sandy level, in a southerly direction. We reached Ayr in the midst of hopeless rain, and drove to the King's Arms Hotel. In the intervals of showers I took peeps at the town, which appeared to have many modern or modern-fronted edifices; altho there are likewise tall, gray, gabled, and quaint-looking houses in the by-streets, here and there, betokening an ancient place. The town lies on both sides of the Ayr, which is here broad and stately, and bordered with dwellings that look from their windows directly down into the passing tide.

I crossed the river by a modern and handsome stone bridge, and recrossed it, at no great distance, by a venerable structure of four gray arches, which must have bestridden the stream ever since

SCOTLAND

the early days of Scottish history. These are the "Two Briggs of Ayr," whose midnight conversation was overheard by Burns, while other auditors were aware only of the rush and rumble of the wintry stream among the arches. The ancient bridge is steep and narrow, and paved like a street, and defended by a parapet of red freestone, except at the two ends, where some mean old shops allow scanty room for the pathway to creep between. . . .

The next morning wore a lowering aspect, as if it felt itself destined to be one of many consecutive days of storm. After a good Scotch breakfast, however, of fresh herrings and eggs, we took a fly, and started at a little past ten for the banks of the Doon. On our way, at about two miles from Ayr, we drew up at a roadside cottage, on which was an inscription to the effect that Robert Burns was born within its walls. It is now a public-house; and, of course, we alighted and entered its little sitting-room, which, as we at present see it, is a neat apartment, with the modern improvement of a ceiling. The walls are much overscribbled with names of visitors, and the wooden door of a cupboard in the wainscot, as well as all the other woodwork of the room, is cut and carved with initial letters. So, likewise, are two tables, which, having received a coat of varnish over the inscriptions, form really curious and interesting articles of furniture. I have seldom (tho I do not personally adopt this mode of illustrating my humble name) felt inclined to ridicule the natural impulse of most people thus to record themselves at the shrines of poets and heroes.

On a panel, let into the wall in a corner of the

room, is a portrait of Burns, copied from the original picture by Nasmyth. The floor of this apartment is of boards, which are probably a recent substitute for the ordinary flag-stones of a peasant's cottage. There is but one other room pertaining to the genuine birthplace of Robert Burns: it is the kitchen, into which we now went. It has a floor of flag-stones, even ruder than those of Shakespeare's house—tho, perhaps, not so strangely cracked and broken as the latter, over which the hoof of Satan himself might seem to have been trampling. A new window has been opened through the wall, toward the road; but on the opposite side is the little original window, of only four small panes, through which came the first daylight that shone upon the Scottish poet. At the side of the room, opposite the fireplace, is a recess, containing a bed, which can be hidden by curtains. In that humble nook, of all places in the world, Providence was pleased to deposit the germ of the richest human life which mankind then had within its circumference.

These two rooms, as I have said, make up the whole sum and substance of Burns's birthplace: for there were no chambers, nor even attics; and the thatched roof formed the only ceiling of kitchen and sitting-room, the height of which was that of the whole house. The cottage, however, is attached to another edifice of the same size and description, as these little habitations often are; and, moreover, a splendid addition has been made to it, since the poet's renown began to draw visitors to the wayside ale-house. The old woman of the house led us through an entry, and showed a vaulted hall, of no vast dimensions, to be sure but marvelously large and splendid as compared with what might be anticipated from the outward aspect of the cottage. It contained a bust of Burns, and was hung round with pictures and engravings, principally illustrative of his life and poems. In this part of the house, too, there is a parlor, fragrant with tobacco-smoke; and, no doubt, many a noggin of whisky is here quaffed to the memory of the bard, who profest to draw so much inspiration from that potent liquor.

We bought some engravings of Kirk Alloway, the Bridge of Doon, and the monument, and gave the old woman a fee besides, and took our leave. A very short drive farther brought us within sight of the monument, and to the hotel, situated close by the entrance of the ornamental grounds within which the former is enclosed. We rang the bell at the gate of the enclosure, but were forced to wait a considerable time; because the old man, the regular superintendent of the spot, had gone to assist at the laying of the corner-stone of a new kirk. He appeared anon, and admitted us, but immediately hurried away to be present at the ceremonies, leaving us locked up with Burns.

The enclosure around the monument is beautifully laid out as an ornamental garden, and abundantly provided with rare flowers and shrubbery, all tended with loving care. The monument stands on an elevated site, and consists of a massive basement-story, three-sided, above which rises a light and elegant Grecian temple—a mere dome, supported on Corinthian pillars, and open to all the winds. The edifice is beautiful in itself; tho I know not what peculiar appropriateness it may have, as the memorial of a Scottish rural poet.

SEEING EUROPE WITH FAMOUS AUTHORS

The door of the basement-story stood open; and, entering, we saw a bust of Burns in a niche, looking keener, more refined, but not so warm and whole-souled as his pictures usually do. I think the likeness can not be good. In the center of the room stood a glass case, in which were deposited the two volumes of the little Pocket Bible that Burns gave to Highland Mary, when they pledged their troth to one another. It is poorly printed, on coarse paper. A verse of Scripture, referring to the solemnity and awfulness of vows, is written within the cover of each volume, in the poet's own hand; and fastened to one of the covers is a lock of Highland Mary's golden hair. This Bible had been carried to America by one of her relatives, but was sent back to be fitly treasured here.

There is a staircase within the monument, by which we ascended to the top, and had a view of both Briggs of Doon; the scene of Tam O'Shanter's misadventure being close at hand. Descending, we wandered through the enclosed garden, and came to a little building in a corner, on entering which, we found the two statues of Tam and Sutor Wat—ponderous stone-work enough, yet permeated in a remarkable degree with living warmth and jovial hilarity. From this part of the garden, too, we again beheld the old Briggs of Doon, over which Tam galloped in such imminent and awful peril. It is a beautiful object in the landscape, with one high, graceful arch, ivy-grown, and shadowed all over and around with foliage.

When we had waited a good while, the old gardener came, telling us that he had heard an excellent prayer at laying the corner-stone of the new kirk. He now gave us some roses and sweetbrier, and let us out from his pleasant garden. We immediately hastened to Kirk Alloway, which is within two or three minutes' walk of the monument. A few steps ascend from the roadside, through a gate, into the old graveyard, in the midst of which stands the kirk. The edifice is wholly roofless, but the side-walls and gable-ends are quite entire, tho portions of them are evidently modern restorations. Never was there a plainer little church, or one with smaller architectural pretension; no New England meeting-house has more simplicity in its very self, tho poetry and fun have clambered and clustered so wildly over Kirk Alloway that it is difficult to see it as it actually exists. By the by, I do not understand why Satan and an assembly of witches should hold their revels within a consecrated precinct; but the weird scene has so established itself in the world's imaginative faith that it must be accepted as an authentic incident, in spite of rule and reason to the contrary. Possibly, some carnal minister, some priest of pious aspect and hidden infidelity, had dispelled the consecration of the holy edifice, by his pretense of prayer, and thus made it the resort of unhappy ghosts and sorcerers and devils.

The interior of the kirk, even now, is applied to quite as impertinent a purpose as when Satan and the witches used it as a dancing-hall; for it is divided in the midst by a wall of stone masonry, and each compartment has been converted into a family burial-place. The name on one of the monuments is Crawfurd; the other bore no inscription. It is impossible not to feel that these good people, whoever they may be, had no business to thrust their prosaic bones into a spot that belongs to the world, and where their presence jars with the emotions, be they sad or gay, which the pilgrim brings thither. They shut us out from our own precincts, too—from that inalienable possession which Burns bestowed in free gift upon mankind, by taking it from the actual earth and annexing it to the domain of imagination.

Kirk Alloway is inconceivably small, considering how large a space it fills in our imagination before we see it. I paced its length, outside of the wall, and found it only seventeen of my paces, and not more than ten of them in breadth. There seem to have been but very few windows, all of which, if I rightly remember, are now blocked up with mason-work of stone. One mullioned window, tall and narrow, in the eastern gable, might have been seen by Tam O'Shanter, blazing with devilish light, as he approached along the road from Ayr; and there is a small and square one, on the side nearest the road, into which he might have peered, as he sat on horseback. Indeed, I could easily have looked through it, standing on the ground, had not the opening been walled up. There is an odd kind of belfry at the peak of one of the gables, with the small bell still hanging in it. And this is all that I remember of Kirk Alloway, except that the stones of its material are gray and irregular.

The road from Ayr passes Alloway Kirk, and crosses the Doon by a modern bridge, without swerving much from a straight line. To reach the old bridge, it appears to have made a bend, shortly after passing the kirk, and then to have turned sharply toward the river. The new bridge is within a minute's walk of the monument; and we went thither, and leaned over its parapet to admire the beautiful Doon, flowing wildly and sweetly between its deep and wooded banks. I never saw a lovelier scene; altho this might have been even lovelier, if a kindly sun had shone upon it. The ivy-grown, ancient bridge, with its high arch, through which we had a picture of the river and the green banks beyond, was absolutely the most picturesque object, in a quiet and gentle way, that ever blest my eyes. Bonny Doon, with its wooded banks, and the boughs dipping into the water! The memory of them, at this moment, affects me like the song of birds, and Burns crooning some verses, simple and wild, in accordance with their native melody. . . . We shall appreciate him better as a poet, hereafter; for there is no writer whose life, as a man, has so much to do with his fame, and throws such a necessary light upon whatever he has produced. Henceforth, there will be a personal warmth for us in everything that he wrote; and, like his countrymen, we shall know him in a kind of personal way, as if we had shaken hands with him, and felt the thrill of his actual voice.

SEEING EUROPE WITH FAMOUS AUTHORS

HIGHLAND MARY'S HOME AND GRAVE*

BY THEODORE F. WOLFE.

There is no stronger proof of the transcending power of the genius of Burns than is found in the fact that, by a bare half-dozen of his stanzas, an humble dairy servant—else unheard of outside her parish and forgotten at her death—is immortalized as a peeress of Petrarch's Laura and Dante's Beatrice, and has been for a century loved and mourned of all the world. We owe much of our tenderest poesy to the heroines whose charms have attuned the fancy and aroused the impassioned muse of enamoured bards; readers have always exhibited a natural avidity to realize the personality of the beings who inspired the tender lays—prompted often by mere curiosity, but more often by a desire to appreciate the tastes and motives of the poets themselves. How little is known of Highland Mary, the most famous heroine of modern song, is shown by the brief, coherent, and often contradictory allusions to her which the biographies of the plowman-poet contain. This paper—prepared during a sojourn in "The Land of Burns"—while it adds a little to our meager knowledge of Mary Campbell, aims to present consecutively and congruously so much as may be known of her brief life, her relation to the bard, and her sad, heroic death.

She first saw the light in 1764, at Ardrossan, on the coast, fifteen miles northward from the "auld

*From "A Literary Pilgrimage." By arrangement with, and by permission of, the publishers, J. B. Lippincott Co. Copyright, 1895.

town of Ayr." Her parentage was of the humblest, her father being a sailor before the mast, and the poor dwelling which sheltered her was in no way superior to the meanest of those we find to-day on the narrow streets of her village. From her birthplace we see, across the Firth of Clyde, the beetling mountains of the Highlands, where she afterward dwelt, and southward the great mass of Ailsa Craig looming, a gigantic pyramid, out of the sea. Mary was named for her aunt, wife of Peter McPherson, a ship-carpenter of Greenock, in whose house Mary died. In her infancy her family removed to the vicinity of Dunoon, on the western shore of the Firth, eight miles below Greenock, leaving the oldest daughter at Ardrossan. Mary grew to young womanhood near Dunoon, then returned to Ayrshire, and found occupation at Coilsfield, near Tarbolton, where her acquaintance with Burns soon began. He told a lady that he first saw Mary while walking in the woods of Coilsfield, and first spoke with her at a rustic merry-making, and, "having the luck to win her regards from other suitors," they speedily became intimate. At this period of life Burns's "eternal propensity to fall into love" was unusually active, even for him, and his passion for Mary (at this time) was one of several which engaged his heart in the interval between the reign of Ellison Begbie—"the lass of the twa sparkling, roguish een"—and that of "Bonnie Jean." Mary subsequently became a servant in the house of Burns's landlord, Gavin Hamilton, a lawyer of Mauchlin, who had early recognized the genius of the bard and admitted him to an intimate friendship, despite his inferior condition. . . .

Within a stone's-throw of Mary dwelt Jean Armour, and when the former returned to Coilsfield, he promptly fell in love with Jean, and solaced himself with her more buxom and compliant charms. It was a year or so later, when his intercourse with Jean had burdened him with grief and shame, that the tender and romantic affection for Mary came into his life. She was yet at Coilsfield, and while he was in hiding—his heart tortured by the apparent perfidy of Jean and all the countryside condemning his misconduct—his intimacy with Mary was renewed; his quickened vision now discerned her endearing attributes, her trust and sympathy were precious in his distress, and awoke in him an affection such as he never felt for any other woman. During a few brief weeks the lovers spent their evenings and Sabbaths together, loitering amid the

"Banks and braes and streams around
The Castle of Montgomery,"

talking of the golden days that were to be theirs when present troubles were past; then came the parting which the world will never forget, and Mary relinquished her service and went to her parents at Campbelltown—a port of Cantyre behind "Arran's mountain isle." Of this parting Burns says, in a letter to Thomson, "We met by appointment on the second Sunday of May, in a sequestered spot on the Ayr, where we spent the day in taking farewell before she should embark for the West Highlands to prepare for our projected change of life." Lovers of Burns linger over this final parting, and detail the impressive

SCOTLAND

ceremonials with which the pair solemnized their bethrothal: they stood on either side of a brook, they laved their hands in the water and scattered it in the air to symbolize the purity of their intentions; clasping hands above an open Bible, they swore to be true to each other forever, then exchanged Bibles, and parted never to meet more.

It is not strange that when death had left him nothing of her but her poor little Bible, a tress of her golden hair, and a tender memory of her love, the recollection of this farewell remained in his soul forever. He has pictured it in the exquisite lines of "Highland Mary" and "To Mary in Heaven." In the monument at Alloway—between the "auld haunted kirk" and the bridge where Maggie lost her tail—we are shown a memento of the parting; it is the Bible which Burns gave to Mary and above which their vows were said. At Mary's death it passed to her sister, at Ardrossan, who bequeathed it to her son William Anderson; subsequently it was carried to America by one of the family, whence it has been recovered to be treasured here. It is a pocket edition in two volumes, to one of which is attached a lock of poor Mary's shining hair. . . .

A visit to the scenes of the brief passion of the pair is a pleasing incident of our Burns pilgrimage. Coilsfield House is somewhat changed since Mary dwelt beneath its roof—a great rambling edifice of gray weather-worn stone with a row of white pillars aligned along its façade, its massive walls embowered in foliage and environed by the grand woods which Burns and Mary knew so well. It was then a seat of Colonel Hugh Montgomerie, a patron of Burns. The name Coilsfield is derived from Coila, the traditional appellation of the district. The grounds comprise a billowy expanse of wood and sward; great reaches of turf, dotted with trees already venerable when the lovers here had their tryst a hundred years ago, slope away from the mansion to the Faile and border its murmuring course to the Ayr. Here we trace with romantic interest the wanderings of the pair during the swift hours of that last day of parting love, their lingering way 'neath the "wild wood's thickening green," by the pebbled shore of Ayr to the brooklet where their vows were made, and thence along the Faile to the woodland shades of Coilsfield, where, at the close of that winged day, "pledging oft to meet again, they tore themselves asunder." Howitt found at Coilsfield a thorn-tree, called by all the country "Highland Mary's thorn," and believed to be the place of final parting; years ago the tree was notched and broken by souvenir seekers; if it be still in existence the present occupant of Coilsfield is unaware. . . . .

Mary remained at Campbeltown during the summer of 1786. Coming to Greenock in the autumn, she found her brother sick of a malignant fever at the house of her aunt; bravely disregarding danger of contagion, she devoted herself to nursing him, and brought him to a safe convalescence only to be herself stricken by his malady and to rapidly sink and die, a sacrifice to her sisterly affection. By this time the success of his poems had determined Burns to remain in Scotland, and he returned to Moss Giel, where tidings of Mary's death reached him. His brother relates that when

SCOTLAND

the letter was handed to him he went to the window and read it, then his face was observed to change suddenly, and he quickly went out without speaking. In June of the next year he made a solitary journey to the Highlands, apparently drawn by memory of Mary. If, indeed, he dropt a tear upon her neglected grave and visited her humble Highland home, we may almost forgive him the excesses of that tour, if not the renewed liaison with Jean which immediately preceded, and the amorous correspondence with "Clarinda" (Mrs. M'Lehose) which followed it. . . . .

Poor Mary is laid in the burial-plot of her uncle in the west kirk-yard of Greenock, near Crawford Street; our pilgrimage in Burns-land may fitly end at her grave. A pathway, beaten by the feet of many reverent visitors, leads us to the spot. It is so pathetically different from the scenes she loved in life—the heather-clad slopes of her Highland home, the seclusion of the wooded braes where she loitered with her poet-lover. Scant foliage is about her; few birds sing above her here. She lies by the wall; narrow streets hem in the enclosure; the air is sullied by smoke from factories and from steamers passing within a stone's throw on the busy Clyde; the clanging of many hammers and the discordant din of machinery and traffic invade the place and sound in our ears as we muse above the ashes of the gentle lassie.

For half a century her grave was unmarked and neglected; then, by subscription, a monument of marble, twelve feet in height, and of graceful proportions, was raised. It bears a sculptured medallion representing Burns and Mary, with clasped hands, plighting their troth. Beneath is the simple inscription, read oft by eyes dim with tears:

> Erected over the grave of
> Highland Mary
> 1842
> "My Mary, dear departed shade,
> Where is thy place of blissful rest?"

THROUGH THE CALEDONIA CANAL TO INVERNESS*

BY HIPPOLYTE ADOLPHE TAINE

In the luminous morning mist, amid a line of masts and rigging, the steamboat sailed down the Clyde to the sea. We proceeded along the indented and rugged coast from one bay to another. These bays, being almost entirely closed in, resemble lakes, and the large sheets of water mirror an amphitheater of green hills. All the corners and windings of the shore are strewn with white villas; the water is crowded with ships; a height was pointed out to me whence three hundred sail may often be counted at a time; a three-decker floats in the distance like a swan among sea-mews. This vast space spread forth and full of life, dilates the mind, one's chest expands more freely, one joyfully inhales the fresh and keen breeze. But the effect upon the nerves and the heart does not resemble that of the Mediterranean; this air and country, instead of pre-disposing to pleasure, dispose to action.

*From "Notes on England." Published by Henry Holt & Co.

SCOTLAND

We enter a small vessel drawn by three horses, which transports us along the Crinan canal, between two banks of green turf. On the one side are rocks covered with brushwood; on the other, steep declivities of a gray or reddish tinge; this, indeed, is color at least, a pleasure for the eye, well mingled, matched, and blended tints. On the bank and amid the bushes are wild roses, and fragile plants with white tufts smile with a delicate and charming grace.

At the outlet from the canal we go on board a large steamer, and the sea opens out wider than ever. The sky is exceedingly clear and brilliant, and the waves break in the sunlight, quivering with reflections of molten tin. The vessel continues her course, leaving in her track a bubbling and boiling path; sea gulls follow unweariedly behind her. On both sides, islands, rocks, boldly-cut promontories stand in sharp relief in the pale azure; the scene changes every quarter of an hour. But on rounding every point the infinite ocean reappears, mingling its almost flat line with the curve of the white sky.

The sun sets, we pass by Glencoe, and Ben Nevis appears sprinkled with snow; the bay becomes narrower, and the mass of water, confined amid barren mountains, assumes a tragic appearance. Human beings have come hither to little purpose. Nature remains indomitable and wild; one feels oneself upon a planet.

We disembark near Fort William; the dying twilight, the fading red rays on the horizon enable us to get a glimpse of a desolate country; acres of peat-bog, eminences rising from the valley between two ranges of huge mountains. A bird of prey screams amid the stillness. Here and there we see some wretched hovels; I am told that those on the heights are dens without windows, and from which the smoke escapes through a hole in the roof. Many of the old men are blind. What an unpropitious abode for man!

On the morrow we voyaged during four hours on the Caledonian canal amidst solitudes, a monotonous row of treeless mountains, enormous green eminences, dotted here and there with fallen stones. A few sheep of a dwarf breed crop the scanty herbage on the slopes; sometimes the winter is so severe that they die; in the distance we perceive a shaggy ox, with savage eyes, the size of a small ass. Both plants and animals perish, or are stunted. In order to make such a land yield anything it must first be replanted with trees, as has been done in Sutherlandshire; a tree renews the soil; it also shelters crops, flocks and herds, and human beings.

The canal terminates in a series of lakes. Nothing is more noble than their aspect, nothing more touching. The water, embrowned by the peat, forms a vast shining plain, surrounded by a circle of mountains. In proportion as we advance each mountain slowly grows upon us, becomes more conspicuous, stands forth with its form and physiognomy; the farther blue peaks melt the one behind the other, diminishing toward the horizon, which they enclose. Thus they stand in position like an assemblage of huge, mournful beings around the black water wherein they are mirrored, while above them and the lake, from time to time, the sun flashes through the shroud of clouds.

At last the solitude becomes less marked. The

SCOTLAND

mountains are half-wooded at first, and then wholly so; they dwindle down; the widening valleys are covered with harvest; the fresh and green verdure of the herbage which supplies forage begins to clothe the hollows and the slopes. We enter Inverness, and we are surprised to find at almost the extreme north of Scotland, on the border of the Highlands, a pretty and lively modern town. It stretches along the two banks of a clear and rapid river. Many houses are newly-built; we note a church, a castle, an iron bridge. In every part are marks of cleanliness, forethought, and special care. The window-panes shine, the frames have been painted; the bell-handles are of copper; there are flowers in the windows; the poorest houses are freshly whitewashed. Well-drest ladies and carefully drest gentlemen walk along the streets. Even a desire to possess works of art is shown by Ionian pillars, specimens of pure Gothic, and other architectural gimcrackery, and these prove at least the search after improvement. The land itself is clearly of inferior quality; industry, order, economy and labor have done everything. How great the contrast between all this and the aspect of a small town on the shores of the Mediterranean, so neglected and filthy, where the lower middle class exist like worms in a worm-eaten beam!

THE SCOTCH HIGHLANDS*

BY HIPPOLYTE ADOLPHE TAINE

On the slopes the violet heaths are spread like a silken carpet under the scanty firs. Higher still are large patches of evergreen wood, and, as soon as the mountain is approached, a brown circle of barren eminences may be discerned toward the horizon. At the end of an hour the desert begins; the climate is inimical to life, even to that of plants. A tarn, the tint of burned topaz, lies coldly and sadly between stony slopes whereon a few tufts of fern and heather grow here and there. Half a league higher is a second tarn, which appears still more dismal in the rising mist. Around, patches of snow are sprinkled on the peaks, and these descending in rivulets produce morasses. The small country ponies, with a sure instinct, surmount the bog, and we arrive at an elevation whence the eye, as far as it can reach, embraces nothing but an amphitheater of desolate, yet green summits; owing to the destruction of timber, everything else has perished; a scene of ruined nature is far more melancholy a spectacle than any human ruins. On our return across the lake, a bag-piper played his instrument. The music is strange and wild, its effects harmonizing with the aspect of the bubbling streams, veined with striking or somber reflections. The same simple note, a kind of dance music, runs through the whole piece in an incorrect and odd manner, and continually recurs, but it is always harsh and rough; it might be likened

*From "Notes on England." Published by Henry Holt & Co.

to an orange shriveled with the cold and rendered bitter.

These are the Highlands. From Braemar to Perth we journey through them for many long miles. It is always a solitude; sometimes five or six valleys in succession are wholly bare, and one may travel for an hour without seeing a tree; then for another hour it is rare merely to see in the distance a wretched twisted birchen-tree, which is dying or dead. It would be some compensation if the rock were naked, and exhibited its mineral structure in all its fulness and ruggedness. But these mountains, of no great elevation, are but bosses with flabby outlines, they have fallen to pieces, and are stone heaps, resembling the remains of a quarry. In winter, torrents of water uproot the heather, leaving on the slopes a leprous, whitened scar, badly tinted by the too feeble sun. The summits are truncated, and want boldness. Patches of miserable verdure seam their sides and mark the oozing of springs; the remainder is covered with brownish heather. Below, at the very bottom, a torrent obstructed by stones, struggles along its channel, or lingers in stagnant pools. One sometimes discerns a hovel, with a stunted cow. The gray, low-lying sky, completes the impression of lugubrious monotony.

Our conveyance ascends the last mountain. At length we see a steep declivity, a great rocky wall; but it is unique. We descend again, and enter a habitable tract. Cultivation occurs first on the lower parts, then on the slopes; the declivities are wooded, and then entire mountains; forests of firs spread their somber mantle over the crests; fields of oats and barley extend on all sides; we perceive pretty clumps of trees, houses surrounded by gardens and flowers, and then culture of all descriptions upon the lessening hills, here and there a park and a modern mansion. The sun bursts forth and shines merrily, but without heat; the fertile plain expands, abounding in promises of convenience and pleasure, and we enter Perth thinking about the historical narrations of Sir Walter Scott, and the contrast between the mountain and the plain, the revilings and scornings interchanged between the inhabitants of the Highlands and the Lowlands.

BEN LOMOND AND THE HIGHLAND LAKES*

BY BAYARD TAYLOR

It was indeed a glorious walk from Dumbarton to Loch Lomond through this enchanting valley. The air was mild and clear; a few light clouds occasionally crossing the sun chequered the hills with sun and shade. I have as yet seen nothing that in pastoral beauty can compare with its glassy winding stream, its mossy old woods and guarding hills and the ivy-grown, castellated towers embosomed in its forests or standing on the banks of the Leven—the purest of rivers. At the little village called Renton is a monument to Smollett, but the inhabitants seem to neglect his memory, as one of the tablets on the pedestal is broken and half fallen away. Farther up the vale a farmer showed

*From "Views Afoot." Published by G. P. Putnam's Sons.

us an old mansion in the midst of a group of trees on the banks of the Leven which he said belonged to Smollett—or Roderick Random, as he called him. Two or three old pear trees were still standing where the garden had formerly been, under which he was accustomed to play in his childhood.

At the head of Leven Vale we set off in the steamer "Watch-Witch" over the crystal waters of Loch Lomond, passing Inch Murrin, the deer-park of the Duke of Montrose, and Inch Caillach,

"where gray pines wave
Their shadows o'er Clan Alpine's grave."

Under the clear sky and golden light of the declining sun we entered the Highlands, and heard on every side names we had learned long ago in the lays of Scott. Here was Glen Fruin and Bannochar, Ross Dhu and the pass of Beal-ma-na. Farther still we passed Rob Roy's rock, where the lake is locked in by lofty mountains. The conelike peak of Ben Lomond rises far above on the right, Ben Voirlich stands in front, and the jagged crest of Ben Arthur looks over the shoulder of the western hills. . . . .

When we arose in the morning, at four o'clock, to return with the boat, the sun was already shining upon the westward hills; scarcely a cloud was in the sky and the air was pure and cool. To our great delight, Ben Lomond was unshrouded, and we were told that a more favorable day for the ascent had not occurred for two months. We left the boat at Rowardennan, an inn, at the southern base of Ben Lomond. After breakfasting on Loch Lomond trout I stole out to the shore while my companions were preparing for the ascent, and made a hasty sketch of the lake.

We proposed descending on the northern side and crossing the Highlands to Loch Katrine; tho it was represented as difficult and dangerous by the guide who wished to accompany us, we determined to run the risk of being enveloped in a cloud on the summit, and so set out alone, the path appearing plain before us. We had no difficulty in following it up the lesser heights, around the base. It wound on over rock and bog, among the heather and broom with which the mountain is covered, sometimes running up a steep acclivity and then winding zigzag round a rocky ascent. The rains two days before had made the bogs damp and muddy; but, with this exception, we had little trouble for some time.

Ben Lomond is a doubly-formed mountain. For about three-fourths of the way there is a continued ascent, when it is suddenly terminated by a large barren plain, from one end of which the summit shoots up abruptly, forming at the north side a precipice five hundred feet high. As we approached the summit of the first part of the mountain the way became very steep and toilsome, but the prospect, which had before been only on the south side, began to open on the east, and we saw suddenly spread out below us the vale of Monteith, with "far Loch Ard and Aberfoil" in the center and the huge front of Ben Venue filling up the picture. Taking courage from this, we hurried on. The heather had become stunted and dwarfish, and the ground was covered with short brown grass. The mountain-sheep which we saw looking at us from the rock above had worn so many paths along the side that we could not tell which to take, but pushed on in the direction of the summit, till, thinking it must be near at hand, we found a mile and a half of plain before us, with the top of Ben Lomond at the farther end. The plain was full of wet moss crossed in all directions by deep ravines or gullies worn in it by the mountain-rains, and the wind swept across with a tempest-like force.

I met near the base a young gentleman from Edinburgh who had left Rowardennan before us, and we commenced ascending together. It was hard work, but neither liked to stop; so we climbed up to the first resting-place, and found the path leading along the brink of a precipice. We soon attained the summit, and, climbing up a little mound of earth and stones, I saw the half of Scotland at a glance. The clouds hung just above the mountain-tops, which rose all around like the waves of a mightly sea. On every side, near and far, stood their misty summits, but Ben Lomond was the monarch of them all. Loch Lomond lay unrolled under my feet like a beautiful map; just opposite, Loch Long thrust its head from between the feet of crowded hills to catch a glimpse of the giant. We could see from Ben Nevis to Ayr—from Edinburgh to Staffa. Stirling and Edinburgh castles would have been visible but that the clouds hung low in the valley of the Forth and hid them from our sight.

. . . At a cottage on the farm of Coman, we procured some oatcakes and milk for dinner from an old Scotch woman who pointed out the direction of Loch Katrine, six miles distant; there was no road, nor, indeed, a solitary dwelling between. The hills were bare of trees, covered with scraggy bushes and rough heath, which in some places was so thick we could scarcely drag our feet through. Added to this, the ground was covered with a kind of moss that retained the moisture like a sponge; so that our boots ere long became thoroughly soaked. Several considerable streams were rushing down the side, and many of the wild breed of black Highland cattle were grazing around. After climbing up and down one or two heights, occasionally startling the moorcock and ptarmigan from their heathery coverts, we saw the valley of Loch Con, while in the middle of the plain on the top of the mountain we had ascended was a sheet of water which we took to be Loch Ackill. Two or three wild-fowl swimming on its surface were the only living things in sight. The peaks around shut it out from all view of the world; a single decayed tree leaned over it from a mossy rock which gave the whole scene an air of the most desolate wildness.

From the next mountain we saw Loch Ackill and Loch Katrine below, but a wet and weary descent had yet to be made. I was about throwing off my knapsack on a rock to take a sketch of Loch Katrine, which appeared to be very beautiful from this point, when we discerned a cavalcade of ponies winding along the path from Inversnaid to the head of the lake, and hastened down to take the boat when they should arrive. . . . As we drew near the eastern end of the lake the scenery became far more beautiful. The Trosachs opened before us. Ben Ledi looked down over the "forehead bare" of Ben An, and as we turned a rocky point Ellen's Isle rose up in front. It is

SCOTLAND

a beautiful little turquoise in the silver setting of Loch Katrine. The northern side alone is accessible, all the others being rocky and perpendicular and thickly grown with trees. We rounded the island to the little bay, bordered by the silver strand, above which is the rock from which Fitz-James wound his horn, and shot under an ancient oak which flung its long gray arms over the water. We here found a flight of rocky steps leading to the top, where stood the bower erected by Lady Willoughby D'Eresby to correspond with Scott's description. Two or three blackened beams are all that remain of it, having been burned down some years ago by the carelessness of a traveler.

The mountains stand all around, like giants, to "sentinel this enchanted land." On leaving the island we saw the Goblin's Cave in the side of Ben Venue, called by the Gaels "Coiran-Uriskin." Near it is Beal-nam-bo—the "Pass of Cattle"—overhung with gray weeping birch-trees.

Here the boatmen stopt to let us hear the fine echo, and the names of Rob Roy and Roderick Dhu were sent back to us apparently at loud as they were given. The description of Scott is wonderfully exact, tho the forest that feathered o'er the sides of Ben Venue has since been cut down and sold by the Duke of Montrose.

When we reached the end of the lake, it commenced raining, and we hastened on through the pass of Beal-an-Duine, scarcely taking time to glance at the scenery, till Loch Achray appeared through the trees, and on its banks the ivy-grown front of the inn of Ardcheancrochan—with its unpronounceable name.

SEEING EUROPE WITH FAMOUS AUTHORS

TO THE HEBRIDES*

BY JAMES BOSWELL.

My acquaintance, the Reverend Mr. John Macauley, one of the ministers of Inverary, and brother to our good friend at Calder, came to us this morning, and accompanied us to the castle, where I presented Dr. Johnson to the Duke of Argyle. We were shown through the house; and I never shall forget the impression made upon my fancy by some of the ladies' maids tripping about in neat morning dresses. After seeing for a long time little but rusticity, their lively manner, and gay, inviting appearance, pleased me so much, that I thought for the moment, I could have been a knight-errant for them.

We then got into a low one-horse chair, ordered for us by the duke, in which we drove about the place. Dr. Johnson was much struck by the grandeur and elegance of this princely seat. He thought, however, the castle too low, and wished it had been a story higher. He said, "What I admire here, is the total defiance of expense." I had a particular pride in showing him a great number of fine old trees, to compensate for the nakedness which had made such an impression on him on the eastern coast of Scotland.

When we came in, before dinner, we found the duke and some gentlemen in the hall. Dr. Johnson took much notice of the large collection of arms, which are excellently disposed there. I told what he had said to Sir Alexander Macdonald,

*From "A Journal of a Tour to the Hebrides with Samuel Johnson, LL.D."

of his ancestors not suffering their arms to rust. "Well," said the doctor, "but let us be glad we live in times when arms may rust. We can sit to-day at his grace's table without any risk of being attacked, and perhaps sitting down again wounded or maimed." The duke placed Dr. Johnson next himself at the table. I was in fine spirits, and tho sensible that I had the misfortune of not being in favor with the duchess I was not in the least disconcerted, and offered her grace some of the dish that was before me. It must be owned that I was in the right to be quite unconcerned, if I could. I was the Duke of Argyle's guest, and I had no reason to suppose that he adopted the prejudices and resentments of the Duchess of Hamilton. . . . .

The duchess was very attentive to Dr. Johnson. I know not how a middle state came to be mentioned. Her Grace wished to hear him on that point. "Madam," said he, "your own relation, Mr. Archibald Campbell, can tell you better about it than I can. He was a bishop of the Nonjuring communion, and wrote a book upon the subject." He engaged to get it for her grace. He afterward gave a full history of Mr. Archibald Campbell, which I am sorry I do not recollect particularly.

He said Mr. Campbell had been bred a violent Whig, but afterward "kept better company, and became a Tory." He said this with a smile, in pleasant allusion, as I thought, to the opposition between his own political principles and those of the duke's clan. He added that Mr. Campbell, after the revolution, was thrown into jail on account of his tenets; but, on application by letter to the old Lord Townshend, was released; that he always spoke of his lordship with great gratitude, saying, "tho a Whig, he had humanity."

A gentleman in company, after dinner, was desired by the duke to go into another room, for a specimen of curious marble, which his grace wished to show us. He brought a wrong piece, upon which the duke sent him back again. He could not refuse, but, to avoid any appearance of servility, he whistled as he walked out of the room, to show his independence. On my mentioning this afterward to Dr. Johnson, he said, it was a nice trait of character.

Dr. Johnson talked a great deal, and was so entertaining, that Lady Betty Hamilton, after dinner, went and placed her chair close to his, leaned upon the back of it, and listened eagerly. It would have made a fine picture to have drawn the sage and her at this time in their several attitudes. He did not know, all the while, how much he was honored. I told him afterward. I never saw him so gentle and complaisant as this day.

We went to tea. The duke and I walked up and down the drawing room, conversing. The duchess still continued to show the same marked coldness for me; for which, tho I suffered from it, I made every allowance, considering the very warm part I had taken for Douglas, in the cause in which she thought her son deeply interested. Had not her grace discovered some displeasure toward me, I should have suspected her of insensibility or dissimulation. . . . .

He was much pleased with our visit at the castle of Inverary. The Duke of Argyle was exceedingly polite to him, and, upon his complaining of the shelties which he had hitherto ridden being too small for him, his grace told him he should be provided with a good horse to carry him next day.

STAFFA AND IONA*

BY WILLIAM HOWITT.

We are bound for the regions of ghosts and fays, mermaids and kelpies, of great sea-snakes, and a hundred other marvels and miracles. To accomplish all this, we have nothing more to do than step on board the steam-packet that lies at the Broomielaw, or great quay at Glasgow. The volume of heavy black smoke, issuing from its nickled chimney, announces that it means to be moving on its way speedily. . . . .

Emerging from the Crinan canal, you issue forth into the Sound of Jura, and feel at once that you are in the stern and yet beautiful region of your youthful admiration. There is the heavy swell and the solemn roar of the great Atlantic. You feel the wild winds that sweep over it. You see around you only high and craggy coasts, that are bleak and naked with the lashings of a thousand tempests. All before you are scattered rocks that emerge from the restless sea, and rocky isles, with patches of the most beautiful greensward, but with scarcely a single tree. The waves are leaping in whiteness against the cliffs, and thousands of sea-birds are floating in long lines on the billows, or skimming past you singly, and diving into the clear

*From "Visits to Remarkable Places."

hissing waters as they near your vessel. One of the very first objects which arrests your senses is the Coryvreckan, or great whirlpool of the Hebrides, an awful feature in all the poetry and ballads belonging to these regions.

I never visited any part of Great Britain which more completely met my anticipated ideas than this. The day was fine, but with a strong breeze. The sea was rough; the wild-fowl were flying, scudding, and diving on all hands; and, wherever the eye turned, were craggy islands—mountains of dark heath or bare splintered stone, and green, solitary slopes, where scarcely a tree or a hut was to be discovered; but now and then black cattle might be descried grazing, or flocks of sheep dotted the hill sides. Far as we could look, were naked rocks rising from the sea, that were worn almost into roundness, or scooped into hollows by the eternal action of the stormy waters. Some of them stood in huge arches, like temples of some shaggy seagod, or haunts of sea-fowl—daylight and the waves passing freely through them. Everywhere were waves, leaping in snowy foam against these rocks and against the craggy shores. It was a stern wilderness of chafing billows and of resisting stone. The rocks were principally of dark red granite, and were cracked across and across, as if by the action of fire or frost. Every thing spake to us of the wild tempests that so frequently rage through these seas. . . . . .

Staffa rose momently in its majesty before us! After all the descriptions which we had read, and the views we had seen of this singular little island, we were struck with delighted astonishment at its aspect. It is, in fact, one great mass of basaltic

SCOTLAND

columns, bearing on their heads another huge mass of black stone, here and there covered with green turf. We sailed past the different caves—the Boat Cave and the Cormorant Cave, which are themselves very wonderful; but it was Fingal's Cave that struck us with admiration and awe. To see this magnificent cavern, with its clustered columns on each side, and pointed arch, with the bleak precipices above it, and the sea raging at its base, and dashing and roaring into its gloomy interior, was worth all the voyage. There are no words that can express the sensation it creates. We were taken in the boats on shore at the northeast point, and landed amid a wilderness of basaltic columns thrown into almost all forms and directions. Some were broken, and lay in heaps in the clear green water. Others were piled up erect and abrupt; some were twisted up into tortuous pyramids at a little distance from the shore itself, and through the passage which they left, the sea came rushing— all foam, and with the most tremendous roar. Others were bent like so many leaden pipes, and turned their broken extremities toward us.

We advanced along a sort of giant's causeway, the pavement of which was the heads of basaltic columns, all fitting together in the most beautiful symmetry; and, turning round the precipice to our right hand, found ourselves at the entrance of the great cave. The sea was too stormy to allow us to enter it, as is often done in boats, we had therefore to clamber along one of its sides, where a row of columns is broken off, at some distance above the waves, and presents an accessible, but certainly very formidable causeway, by which you may reach the far end. I do not believe that any stranger, if he were there alone, would dare to pass along that irregular and slippery causeway, and penetrate to the obscure end of the cave; but numbers animate one another to anything. We clambered along this causeway or corridor, now ascending and now descending, as the broken columns required, and soon stood—upward of seventy of us—ranged along its side from one end to the other. Let it be remembered that this splendid sea cave is forty-two feet wide at the entrance; sixty-six feet high from low water; and runs into the rock two hundred and twenty-seven feet. Let it be imagined that at eight or ten feet below us it was paved with the sea, which came rushing and foaming along it, and dashing up against the solid rock at its termination; while the light thrown from the flickering billows quivered in its arched roof above us, and the whole place was filled with the solemn sound of the ocean; and if any one can imagine to himself any situation more sublime, I should like to know what that is. The roof is composed of the lower ends of basaltic columns, which have yet been so cut away by nature as to give it the aspect of the roof of some gigantic cathedral aisle; and lichens of gold and crimson have gilded and colored it in the richest manner.

It was difficult to forget, as we stood there, that, if any one slipt, he would disappear forever, for the billows in their ebb would sweep him out to the open sea, as it were in a moment. Yet the excitement of the whole group was too evident to rest with any seriousness on such a thought. Some one suddenly fired a gun in the place, and the concussion and reverberated thunders were astounding.

SCOTLAND

When the first effect was gone off, one general peal of laughter rung through the cave, and then nearly the whole company began to sing "The Sea! the sea!" The captain found it a difficult matter to get his company out of this strange chantry—where they and the wind and waves seemed all going mad together—to embark them again for Iona.

Venerable Iona—how different! and with what different feelings approached! As we drew near, we saw a low bleak shore, backed by naked hills, and at their feet a row of miserable Highland huts, and at separate intervals the ruins of the monastery and church of Ronad, the church of St. Oran and its burying-ground, and lastly, the cathedral. . . . .

Nothing is more striking, in this wild and neglected spot, than to walk among these ruins, and behold amid the rank grass those tombs of ancient kings, chiefs, and churchmen, with their sculpture of so singular and yet superior a style. It is said that there were formerly three hundred and sixty stone crosses in the Island of Iona, which since the Reformation have been reduced to two, and the fragments of two others. The Synod of Argyle is reported to have caused no less than sixty of them to be thrown into the sea at one time, and fragments of others, which were knocked in pieces, are to be seen here and there, some of them now converted into gravestones.

They lie on the margin of the stormy Atlantic; they lie among walls which, tho they may be loosened for years, seem as tho they never could decay, for they are of the red granite of which the rocks and islets around are composed, and defended only by low enclosures piled up of the same granite, rounded into great pebbles by the washing of the sea. But perhaps the most striking scene of all was our own company of voyagers landing amid the huge masses of rock that scatter the strand; forming into long procession, two and two, and advancing in that order from one ruin to another.

We chanced to linger behind for a moment; and our eye caught this procession of upward of seventy persons thus wandering on amid those time-worn edifices—and here and there a solitary cross lifting its head above them. It was a picture worthy of a great painter. It looked as tho the day of pilgrimages was come back again, and that this was a troop of devotees thronging to this holy shrine. The day of pilgrimages is, indeed come back again; but they are the pilgrimages of knowledge and an enlightened curiosity. The day of that science which the saints of Iona were said to diffuse first in Britain has now risen to a splendid noon; and not the least of its evidences is that, every few days through every summer, a company like this descends on this barren strand to behold what Johnson calls "that illustrious island which was once the luminary of the Caledonian regions, whence savage clans and roving barbarians derived the benefit of knowledge and the blessings of religion." A more interesting or laudable excursion the power of steam and English money can not well enable our countrymen to make.

VII

IRELAND

A SUMMER DAY IN DUBLIN*

BY WILLIAM MAKEPEACE THACKERAY

Our passage across from the Head [Holyhead] was made in a rain so pouring and steady, that sea and coast were entirely hidden from us, and one could see very little beyond the glowing tip of the cigar which remained alight nobly in spite of the weather. When the gallant exertions of that fiery spirit were over for ever, and, burning bravely to the end, it had breathed its last in doing its master service, all became black and cheerless around; the passengers had dropt off one by one, preferring to be dry and ill below rather than wet and squeamish above; even the mate, with his gold-laced cap (who is so astonishingly like Mr. Charles Dickens, that he might pass for that gentleman)—even the mate said he would go to his cabin and turn in. So there remained nothing for it but to do as all the world had done. . . .

A long pier, with a steamer or two at hand, and a few small vessels lying on either side of the jetty; a town irregularly built, with showy-looking hotels; a few people straggling on the beach; two or three cars at the railroad

*From "The Irish Sketch Book."

station, which runs along the shore as far as Dublin; the sea stretching interminably eastward; to the north the Hill of Howth, lying gray behind the mist; and, directly under his feet, upon the wet, black, shining, slippery deck, an agreeable reflection of his own legs, disappearing seemingly in the direction of the cabin from which he issues; are the sights which a traveler may remark on coming on deck at Kingstown pier on a wet morning—let us say on an average morning; for according to the statement of well-informed natives, the Irish day is more often rainy than otherwise. A hideous obelisk, stuck upon four fat balls, and surmounted with a crown on a cushion (the latter were no bad emblems perhaps of the monarch in whose honor they were raised), commemorates the sacred spot at which George IV. quitted Ireland: you are landed here from the steamer; and a carman, who is dawdling in the neighborhood, with a straw in his mouth, comes leisurely up to ask whether you'll go to Dublin?

Is it natural indolence, or the effect of despair because of the neighboring railroad, which renders him so indifferent? He does not even take the straw out of his mouth as he proposes the question, and seems quite careless as to the answer. He said he would take me to Dublin "in three quarthers," as soon as we began a parley; as to the fare, he would not hear of it—he said he would leave it to my honor; he would take me for nothing. Was it possible to refuse such a genteel offer?

Before that day, so memorable for joy and sorrow, for rapture at receiving its monarch and tearful grief at losing him, when George IV. came and left the maritime resort of the citizens of Dublin, it bore a less genteel name than that which it owns at present, and was called Dunleary. After that glorious event Dunleary disdained to be Dunleary any longer, and became Kingstown henceforward and forever. Numerous terraces and pleasure-houses have been built in the place —they stretch row after row along the banks of the sea, and rise one above another on the hill. The rents of these houses are said to be very high; the Dublin citizens crowd into them in summer; and a great source of pleasure and comfort must it be to them to have the fresh sea-breezes and prospects so near to the metropolis.

The better sort of houses are handsome and spacious; but the fashionable quarter is yet in an unfinished state, for enterprising architects are always beginning new roads, rows and terraces; nor are those already built by any means complete.* Besides the aristocratic part of the town is a commercial one, and nearer to Dublin stretch lines of low cottages which have not a Kingstown look at all, but are evidently of the Dunleary period. . . . The capabilities of the country, however, are very, very great, and in many instances have been taken advantage of; for you see, besides the misery, numerous handsome houses and parks along the road, having fine lawns and woods, and the sea in our view, at a quarter of an hour's ride from Dublin. It is the continual appearance of this sort of wealth which makes the poverty more striking; and thus between the two (for there is no vacant space of fields be-

*This was written in 1842.

tween Kingstown and Dublin) the car reaches the city.

The entrance to the capital is very handsome. There is no bustle and throng of carriages, as in London; but you pass by numerous rows of neat houses, fronted with gardens, and adorned with all sorts of gay-looking creepers. Pretty market-gardens, with trim beds of plants and shining glass-houses, give the suburbs a riante and cheerful look; and, passing under the arch of the railway, we are in the city itself. Hence you come upon several old-fashioned, well-built, airy, stately streets, and through Fitzwilliam Square, a noble place, the garden of which is full of flowers and foliage. The leaves are green, and not black as in similar places in London; the red-brick houses tall and handsome. Presently the car stops before an extremely big red house, in that extremely large square, Stephen's Green, where Mr. O'Connell says there is one day or other to be a Parliament. There is room enough for that, or for any other edifice which fancy or patriotism may have a mind to erect, for part of one of the sides of the square is not yet built, and you see the fields and the country beyond. . . .

The hotel to which I had been directed is a respectable old edifice, much frequented by families from the country, and where the solitary traveler may likewise find society. For he may either use the Shelburne as a hotel or a boarding-house, in which latter case he is comfortably accommodated at the very moderate daily charge. For this charge a copious breakfast is provided for him in the coffee-room, a perpetual luncheon is likewise there spread, a

IRELAND

plentiful dinner is ready at six o'clock; after which, there is a drawing-room and a rubber of whist, with tay and coffee and cakes in plenty to satisfy the largest appetite. The hotel is majestically conducted by clerks and other officers; the landlord himself does not appear, after the honest comfortable English fashion, but lives in a private mansion hard by, where his name may be read inscribed on a brass-plate, like that of any other private gentleman.

A woman melodiously crying "Dublin Bay herrings" passed just as we came up to the door, and as that fish is famous throughout Europe, I seized the earliest opportunity and ordered a broiled one for breakfast. It merits all its reputation: and in this respect I should think the Bay of Dublin is far superior to its rival of Naples. Are there any herrings in Naples Bay? Dolphins there may be; and Mount Vesuvius, to be sure, is bigger than even the Hill of Howth: but a dolphin is better in a sonnet than at a breakfast, and what poet is there that, at certain periods of the day, would hesitate in his choice between the two?

With this famous broiled herring the morning papers are served up; and a great part of these, too, gives opportunity of reflection to the newcomer, and shows him how different this country is from his own. Some hundred years hence, when students want to inform themselves of the history of the present day, and refer to files of "Times" and "Chronicle" for the purpose, I think it is possible that they will consult, not so much those luminous and philosophical leading articles which call our attention at present both by the majesty of their eloquence and the largeness of their type, but that they will turn to those parts of the journals into which information is squeezed into the smallest possible print, to the advertisements, namely, the law and police reports, and to the instructive narratives supplied by that ill-used body of men who transcribe knowledge at the rate of a penny a line. . . . .

The papers being read, it became my duty to discover the town; and a handsomer town, with fewer people in it, it is impossible to see on a summer's day. In the whole wide square of Stephen's Green, I think there were not more than two nursery-maids, to keep company with the statue of George I., who rides on horseback in the middle of the garden, the horse having his foot up to trot, as if he wanted to go out of town too. Small troops of dirty children (too poor and dirty to have lodgings at Kingstown) were squatting here and there upon the sunshiny steps, the only clients at the thresholds of the professional gentlemen whose names figure on brass-plates on the doors. A stand of lazy carmen, a policeman or two with clinking boot-heels, a couple of moaning beggars leaning against the rails and calling upon the Lord, and a fellow with a toy and book stall, where the lives of St. Patrick, Robert Emmet, and Lord Edward Fitzgerald may be bought for double their value, were all the population of the Green. . . . . In the courts of the College, scarce the ghost of a gyp or the shadow of a bed-maker. In spite of the solitude, the square of the College is a fine sight—a large ground, surrounded by buildings of various ages and styles, but comfortable, handsome, and in

IRELAND

good repair; a modern row of rooms; a row that has been Elizabethan once; a hall and senate-house, facing each other, of the style of George I.; and a noble library, with a range of many windows, and a fine manly simple façade of cut stone.

The bank and other public buildings of Dublin are justly famous. In the former may still be seen the room which was the House of Lords formerly, and where the bank directors now sit, under a clean marble image of George III. The House of Commons has disappeared, for the accommodation of clerks and cashiers. The interior is light, splendid, airy, well furnished, and the outside of the building not less so. The Exchange, hard by, is an equally magnificent structure; but the genius of commerce has deserted it, for all its architectural beauty. There was nobody inside when I entered, but a pert statue of George III. in a Roman toga, simpering and turning out his toes; and two dirty children playing, whose hoop-sticks caused great clattering echoes under the vacant sounding dome.

Walking toward the river, you have on either side of you, at Carlisle Bridge, a very brilliant and beautiful prospect. The four courts and their dome to the left, the custom-house and its dome to the right; and in this direction seaward, a considerable number of vessels are moored, and the quays are black and busy with the cargoes discharged from ships. Seamen cheering, herring-women bawling, coal-carts loading—the scene is animated and lively. Yonder is the famous Corn Exchange; but the Lord Mayor is attending to his duties in Parliament, and little of note is going on. I had just passed his lordship's mansion in Dawson Street—a queer old dirty brick house, with dumpy urns at each extremity, and looking as if a story of it had been cut off—a rasée house. Close at hand, and peering over a paling, is a statue of our blest sovereign George II. How absurd these pompous images look, of defunct majesties, for whom no breathing soul cares a halfpenny! It is not so with the effigy of William III., who has done something to merit a statue. At this minute the Lord Mayor has William's effigy under a canvas, and is painting him of a bright green picked out with yellow—his lordship's own livery.

The view along the quays to the four courts has no small resemblance to a view along the quays at Paris, tho not so lively as are even those quiet walks. The vessels do not come above-bridge, and the marine population remains constant about them, and about numerous dirty liquor-shops, eating-houses, and marine-store establishments, which are kept for their accommodation along the quay. As far as you can see, the shining Liffey flows away eastward, hastening (like the rest of the inhabitants of Dublin) to the sea.

In front of Carlisle Bridge, and not in the least crowded, tho in the midst of Sackville Street, stands Nelson upon a stone pillar. The postoffice is on his right hand (only it is cut off); and on his left, Gresham's and the Imperial Hotel. Of the latter let me say (from subsequent experience) that it is ornamented by a cook who could dress a dinner by the side of M. Borel or M. Soyé. Would there were more such artists in this ill-fated country! The street is exceedingly broad and handsome; the shops at the commencement, rich and spacious; but in Upper Sackville Street, which closes with the pretty building and gardens of the Rotunda, the appearance of wealth begins to fade somewhat, and the houses look as if they had seen better days. Even in this, the great street of the town, there is scarcely any one, and it is as vacant and listless as Pall Mall in October.

DUBLIN CASTLE*

BY MR. AND MRS. S. C. HALL

The building of Dublin "Castle"—for the residence of the Viceroys retains the term—was commenced by Meiler FitzHenry, Lord Justice of Ireland, in 1205; and finished, fifteen years afterward, by Henry de Loundres, Archbishop of Dublin. The purpose of the structure is declared by the patent by which King John commanded its erection: "You have given us to understand that you have not a convenient place wherein our treasure may be safely deposited; and forasmuch, as well for that use as for many others, a fortress would be necessary for us at Dublin, we command you to erect a castle there, in such competent place as you shall judge most expedient, as well to curb the city as to defend it if occasion shall so require, and that you make it as strong as you can with good and durable walls." Accordingly it was occupied as a strong

*From "Ireland: Its Scenery, Character, Etc."

fortress only, until the reign of Elizabeth, when it became the seat of the Irish government—the court being held previously at various palaces in the city or its suburbs; and in the seventeenth century, Terms and Parliaments were both held within its walls.

The Castle, however, has undergone so many and such various changes from time to time, as circumstances justified the withdrawal of its defenses, that the only portion of it which nows bears a character of antiquity is the Birmingham Tower; and even that has been almost entirely rebuilt, altho it retains its ancient form. The records of this tower—in modern times the "State Paper Office"—would afford materials for one of the most singular and romantic histories ever published. It received its name, according to Dr. Walsh, not from the De Birminghams, who were lords justices in 1321 and 1348; but from Sir William Birmingham, who was imprisoned there in 1331, with his son Walter; "the former was taken out from thence and executed, the latter was pardoned as to life because he was in holy orders." It was the ancient keep, or ballium, of the fortress; and was for a very long period the great state prison, in which were confined the resolute or obstinate Milesian chiefs, and the rebellious Anglo-Norman lords. Strong and well guarded as it was, however, its inmates contrived occasionally to escape from its durance. Some of the escapes which the historians have recorded are remarkable and interesting.

The Castle is situated on very high ground, nearly in the center of the city; the principal

IRELAND

entrance is by a handsome gateway. The several buildings, surrounding two squares, consist of the lord-lieutenant's state apartments, guard-rooms, the offices of the chief secretary, the apartments of aides-du-camp and officers of the household, the offices of the treasury, hanaper, register, auditor-general, constabulary, etc., etc. The buildings have a dull and heavy character—no effort has been made at elegance or display—and however well calculated they may seem for business, the whole have more the aspect of a prison than a court. There is, indeed, one structure that contributes somewhat to redeem the somber appearance of "the Castle"—the chapel is a fine Gothic edifice, richly decorated both within and without. The following description of the ancient character of "the Castle" is gathered from Dr. Walsh:

"The entrance from the city on the north side was by a drawbridge, placed between two strong round towers from Castle Street, the westward of which subsisted till the year 1766. A portcullis, armed with iron, between these towers, served as a second defense, in case the bridge should be surprised by an enemy. A high curtain extended from the western tower to Cork Tower, so called after the great Earl of Cork, who, in 1624, expended a considerable sum in rebuilding it. The wall was then continued of equal height until it joined Birmingham Tower, which was afterward used as a prison for state criminals; it was taken down in 1775, and the present building erected on the site, for preserving part of the ancient records of the kingdom. From this another high curtain extended to the Wardrobe Tower, which served as repository for the royal robe, the cap of maintenance, and the other furniture of state. From this tower the wall was carried to the North or Storehouse Tower (now demolished) near Dame's Gate, and from thence it was continued to the eastern gateway tower, at the entrance of the castle. This fortress was originally encompassed with a broad and deep moat, which has long since been filled up. There were two sally ports in the wall, one toward Sheep (now Ship) Street, which was closed up in 1663 by the Duke of Ormond, after the discovery of Jephson and Blood's conspiracy."

The walls by which it was formerly surrounded, and the fortifications for its defense, have nearly all vanished. Neither is Dublin rich in remains of antiquity; one of the few that appertain to its ancient history is a picturesque gateway, but not of a very remote date, called Marsh's Gate. It stands in Kevin Street, near the cathedral of St. Patrick, and is the entrance to a large court, now occupied by the horse police; at one end of which is the Barrack, formerly, we believe, the Deanery, and Marsh's library.

ST. PATRICK'S CATHEDRAL*

BY MR. AND MRS. S. C. HALL

If few of the public structures of Dublin possess "the beauty of age," many of its churches may be classed with the "ancient of days." Chief among them all is the Cathedral of St.

*From "Ireland: Its Scenery, Character, Etc."

IRELAND

Patrick; interesting, not alone from its antiquity, but from its association with the several leading events, and remarkable people, by which and by whom Ireland has been made "famous." It is situated in a very old part of Dublin, in the midst of low streets and alleys, the houses being close to the small open yard by which the venerable structure is encompassed. Its condition, too, is very wretched; and altho various suggestions have been made, from time to time, for its repair and renovation, it continues in a state by no means creditable either to the church or the city. It was built A.D. 1190, by John Comyn, Archbishop of Dublin, by whom it was dedicated to the patron saint of Ireland; but it is said, the site on which it stands was formerly occupied by a church erected by the saint himself—A.D. 448. St. Patrick's was collegiate in its first institution, and erected into a cathedral about the year 1225, by Henry de Loundres, successor to Archbishop Comyn, "united with the cathedral of the Holy Trinity, Christ's Church, Dublin, into one spouse, saving unto the latter the prerogative of honor." The question of precedence between the sees of Dublin and Armagh was agitated for centuries with the greatest violence, and both pleaded authority in support of their pretensions; it was at length determined, in 1552, that each should be entitled to primatial dignity, and erect his crozier in the diocese of the other: that the archbishop of Dublin should be titled the "Primate of Ireland;" while the archbishop of Armagh should be styled, with more precision, "Primate of all Ireland"—a distinction which continues to the present day.

Above two centuries before this arrangement, however, as the diocese of Dublin contained two cathedrals—St. Patrick's and Christ Church—an agreement was made between the chapters of both, that each church should be called Cathedral and Metropolitan, but that Christ Church should have precedence, as being the elder church, and that the archbishops should be buried alternately in the two cathedrals.

The sweeping censure of Sir Richard Colt Hoare, that "in point of good architecture it has little to notice or commend," is not to be questioned; ruins—and, in its present state, St. Patrick's approaches very near to be classed among them—of far greater beauty abound in Ireland. It is to its associations with the past that the cathedral is mainly indebted for its interest. The choral music of St. Patrick's is said to be "almost unrivalled for its combined powers of voice, organ, and scientific skill."

LIMERICK*

BY MR. AND MRS. S. C. HALL

Limerick is distinguished in history as "the city of the violated treaty;" and the Shannon, on which it stands, has been aptly termed "the King of Island Rivers." Few of the Irish counties possess so many attractions for the antiquarian and the lover of the picturesque: and with one exception, no city of Ireland has con-

*From "Ireland: Its Scenery, Character, Etc."

tributed so largely to maintain the honor and glory of the country. The brave defenders of Limerick and Londonderry have received—the former from the Protestant, and the latter from the Catholic, historian—the praise that party spirit failed to weaken; the heroic gallantry, the indomitable perseverance, and the patient and resolute endurance under suffering, of both, having deprived political partizans of their asperity —compelling them, for once at least, to render justice to their opponents; all having readily subscribed to the opinion that "Derry and Limerick will ever grace the historic page, as rival companions and monuments of Irish bravery, generosity, and integrity."

From a very early period Limerick has held rank among the cities of Ireland, second only to that of the capital; and before its walls were defeated, first, the Anglo-Norman chivalry; next, the sturdy Ironsides of Cromwell; and last, the victorious army of William the Third. Like most of the Irish sea-ports, it was, in the ninth and tenth centuries, a settlement of the Danes, between whom and the native Irish many encounters took place, until finally the race of the sea-kings was expelled from the country.

It is certain that at this early period Limerick was a place of considerable importance; for some time after, indeed until the conquest by the English, it was the capital of the province, and the seat of the kings of Thomond, or North Munster, who were hence called Kings of Limerick. Upon the arrival of Strongbow, Donnell O'Brien swore fealty to Henry the Second, but subsequently revolted; and Raymond Le Gros, the bravest and noblest of all the followers of Strongbow, laid siege to his city. Limerick was at that time "environed with a foule and deepe ditch with running water, not to be passed over without boats, but by one foord only;" the English soldiers were therefore discouraged, and would have abandoned the attempt to take it, but that "a valiaunt knight, Meyler Fitz-Henry, having found the foord, wyth a loud voyce cried 'St. David, companions, let us corageouslie pass this foord.'" For some years after the city was alternately in the possession of the English and the Irish; on the death of Strongbow, it was surrendered to the keeping of its native prince, who swore to govern it for the King of England; but the British knights had scarcely passed the bridge, when he destroyed it and set fire to the town.

After again repeatedly changing hands, it was finally settled by the renowned William de Burgo, ancestor of the present Marquis of Clanricarde, and remained an appanage to the English crown. At this period, and for some time after, Limerick, was "next in consequence" to Dublin. Richard the First, in the ninth year of his reign, granted it a charter to elect a mayor—an honor which London did not then enjoy, and which Dublin did not receive until a century later; and King John, according to Stanihurst, was "so pleased with the agreeableness of the city, that he caused a very fine castle and bridge to be built there." The castle has endured for above six centuries; in all the "battles, sieges, fortunes," that have since occurred, it has been the object most coveted, perhaps in Ireland, by the contending parties; and it still frowns, a dark mass, upon the waters of the mighty Shannon.

The great attraction of Limerick—altho by no means the only one—is, however, its majestic and beautiful river: "the king of island rivers,"—the "principallest of all in Ireland," writes the quaint old naturalist, Dr. Gerrard Boate. It takes its rise among the mountains of Leitrim—strange to say, the precise spot has not been ascertained—and running for a few miles as an inconsiderable stream, diffuses itself into a spacious lake, called Lough Allyn. Issuing thence it pursues its course for several miles, and forms another small lake, Lough Eike; again spreads itself out into Lough Ree,—a lake fifteen miles in length and four in breadth; and thence proceeds as a broad and rapid river, passing by Athlone; then narrowing again until it reaches Shannon harbor; then widening into far-famed Lough Derg, eighteen miles long and four broad; then progressing until it arrives at Killaloe, where it ceases to be navigable until it waters Limerick city; from whence it flows in a broad and majestic volume to the ocean for about sixty miles; running a distance of upward of 200 miles from its source to its mouth—between Loop Head and Kerry Head (the space between them being about eight miles), watering ten counties in its progress, and affording facilities for commerce and internal intercourse such as are unparalleled in any other portion of the United Kingdom.

"The spacious Shenan spreading like a sea," thus answers to the description of Spenser; for a long space its course is so gentle that ancient writers supposed its name to have been derived from "Seen-awn," the slow river; and for many miles, between O'Brien's Bridge and Limerick, it rolls so rapidly along as almost to be characterized as a series of cataracts. At the falls of Killaloe, it descends twenty-one feet in a mile; and above one hundred feet from Killaloe to Limerick. . . . . Its banks too are, nearly all along its course, of surpassing beauty; as it nears Limerick, the adjacent hills are crowned with villas; and upon its sides are the ruins of many ancient castles. Castle Connell, a village about six miles from the city, is perhaps unrivaled in the kingdom for natural graces; and immediately below it are the Falls of Doonas where the river rushes over huge mountain-rocks, affording a passage which the more daring only will make; for the current—narrowed to a boat's breadth—rushes along with such frightful rapidity, that the deviation of a few inches would be inevitable destruction.

The immediate environs of Limerick are not picturesque; the city lies in a spacious plain, the greater portion of which is scarcely above the level of the water: at short distances, however, there are some of the most interesting ruins in the kingdom, in the midst of scenery of surpassing loveliness. Of these, the tourist should first visit Carrig-o-gunnel, next Adare, and then Castle Connell, the most beautiful of many beautiful places upon the banks of the noble Shannon.

IRELAND

FROM BELFAST TO DUBLIN*

BY WILLIAM CULLEN BRYANT

We left Glasgow on the morning of the 22d, and taking the railway to Ardrossan were soon at the beach. One of those iron steamers which navigate the British waters, far inferior to our own in commodious and comfortable arrangements, but strong and safe, received us on board, and at ten o'clock we were on our way to Belfast.

The coast of Ayr, with the cliff near the birthplace of Burns, continued long in sight; we passed near the mountains of Arran, high and bare steeps swelling out of the sea, which had a look of almost complete solitude; and at length Ailsa Craig began faintly to show itself, high above the horizon, through the thick atmosphere.

We passed this lonely rock, about which flocks of sea-birds, the solan goose, and the gannet, on long white wings with jetty tips, were continually wheeling, and with a glass we could discern them sitting by thousands on the shelves of the rock, where they breed. The upper part of Ailsa, above the cliffs which reach more than half-way to the summit, appears not to be destitute of soil, for it was tinged with a faint verdure.

In about nine hours we had crossed the channel, over smooth water, and were making our way, between green shores almost without a tree,

*From "Letters of a Traveler."

up the bay, at the bottom of which stands, or rather lies, for its site is low, the town of Belfast. We had yet enough of daylight left to explore a part at least of the city. "It looks like Albany," said my companion, and really the place bears some resemblance to the streets of Albany which are situated near the river, nor is it without an appearance of commercial activity.

The people of Belfast, you know, are of Scotch origin, with some infusion of the original race of Ireland. I heard English spoken with a Scotch accent, but I was obliged to own that the severity of the Scotch physiognomy had been softened by the migration and the mingling of breed. . . . At an early hour the next day we were in our seats on the outside of the mail-coach. We passed through a well-cultivated country, interspersed with towns which had an appearance of activity and thrift. The dwellings of the cottagers looked more comfortable than those of the same class in Scotland, and we were struck with the good looks of the people, men and women, whom we passed in great numbers going to their work.

At length, having traversed the county of Down, we entered Louth. . . . . Close on the confines of Armagh, perhaps partly within it, we traversed, near the village of Jonesborough, a valley full of the habitations of peat-diggers. Its aspect was most remarkable, the barren hills that inclose it were dark with heath and gorse and with ledges of brown rock, and their lower declivities, as well as the level of the valley, black with peat, which had been cut from the ground and laid in rows.

IRELAND

The men were at work with spades cutting it from the soil, and the women were pressing the water from the portions thus separated, and exposing it to the air to dry. .... It is the property of peat earth to absorb a large quantity of water, and to part with it slowly. The springs, therefore, in a region abounding with peat make no brooks; the water passes into spongy soil and remains there, forming morasses even on the slopes of the hills.

As we passed out of this black valley we entered a kind of glen, and the guard, a man in a laced hat and scarlet coat, pointed to the left, and said, "There is a pretty place." It was a beautiful park along a hill-side, groves and lawns, a broad domain, jealously inclosed by a thick and high wall, beyond which we had, through the trees, a glimpse of a stately mansion.

Our guard was a genuine Irishman, strongly resembling the late actor Power in physiognomy, with the very brogue which Power sometimes gave to his personages. He was a man of pithy speech, communicative, and acquainted apparently with everybody of every class, whom we passed on the road. Besides him we had for fellow-passengers three very intelligent Irishmen, on their way to Dublin. One of them was a tall, handsome gentleman, with dark hair and hazel eyes, and a rich South-Irish brogue. He was fond of his joke, but next to him sat a graver personage, in spectacles, equally tall, with fair hair and light-blue eyes, speaking with a decided Scotch accent. By my side was a square-built, fresh-colored personage, who had traveled in America, and whose accent was almost English. I thought I could not be mistaken in supposing them to be samples of the three different races by which Ireland is peopled.

We now entered a fertile district, meadows heavy with grass, in which the haymakers were at work, and fields of wheat and barley as fine as I had ever seen. . . . One or two green mounds stood close to the road, and we saw others at a distance.

"They are Danish forts," said the guard.

"Every thing we do not know the history of, we put upon the Danes," added the South of Ireland man.

These grassy mounds, which are from ten to twenty feet in height, are now supposed to have been the burial places of the ancient Celts. The peasantry can with difficulty be persuaded to open any of them, on acount of a prevalent superstition that it will bring bad luck.

A little before we arrived at Drogheda, I saw a tower to the right, apparently a hundred feet in height, with a doorway at a great distance from the ground, and a summit somewhat dilapidated.

"That is one of the round towers of Ireland, concerning which there is so much discussion," said my English-looking fellow-traveler.

These round towers, as the Dublin antiquarians tell me, were probably built by the early Christian missionaries from Italy, about the seventh century, and were used as places of retreat and defense against the pagans.

Not far from Drogheda, I saw at a distance a quiet-looking valley.

IRELAND

"That," said the English-looking passenger, "is the valley of the Boyne, and in that spot was fought the famous battle of the Boyne."

"Which the Irish are fighting about yet, in America," added the South of Ireland man.

They pointed out near the spot, a cluster of trees on an eminence, where James beheld the defeat of his followers. We crossed the Boyne, entered Drogheda, dismounted among a crowd of beggars, took our places in the most elegant railway wagon we had ever seen, and in an hour were set down in Dublin. . . . . I have seen no loftier nor more spacious dwellings than those which overlook St. Stephen's Green, a noble park, planted with trees, under which this showery sky and mild temperature maintain a verdure all the year, even in mid-winter. About Merrion square, another park, the houses have scarcely a less stately appearance, and one of these with a strong broad balcony, from which to address the people in the street, is inhabited by O'Connell. The park of the University, in the midst of the city, is of great extent, and the beautiful public grounds called Phenix Park, have a circumference of eight miles.

SEEING EUROPE WITH FAMOUS AUTHORS

THE GIANT'S CAUSEWAY*

BY BAYARD TAYLOR

We passed the Giant's Causeway after dark, and about eleven o'clock reached the harbor of Port Rush, where, after stumbling up a strange old street in the dark, we found a little inn, and soon forgot the Irish coast and everything else.

In the morning, when we arose, it was raining, with little prospect of fair weather, but having expected nothing better, we set out on foot for the Causeway. The rain, however, soon came down in torrents, and we were obliged to take shelter in a cabin by the roadside. The whole house consisted of one room with bare walls and roof and earthen floor, while a window of three or four panes supplied the light. A fire of peat was burning on the hearth, and their breakast, of potatoes alone, stood on the table. The occupants received us with rude but genuine hospitality, giving us the only seats in the room to sit upon; except a rickety bedstead that stood in one corner and a small table, there was no other furniture in the house. The man appeared rather intelligent, and, altho he complained of the hardness of their lot, had no sympathy with O'Connell or the Repeal movement.

We left this miserable hut as soon as it ceased raining, and, tho there were many cabins along the road, few were better than this. At length, after passing the walls of an old church in the midst of older tombs, we saw the roofless

*From "Views Afoot." Published by G. P. Putnam's Sons.

IRELAND

towers of Dunluce Castle on the seashore. It stands on an isolated rock, rising perpendicularly two hundred feet above the sea, and connected with the cliffs of the mainland by a narrow arch.

We left the road near Dunluce and walked along the smooth beach to the cliffs that surround the Causeway. Here we obtained a guide, and descended to one of the caves which can be entered from the shore. Opposite the entrance a bare rock called Sea Gull Isle rises out of the sea like a church-steeple. The roof at first was low, but we shortly came to a branch that opened on the sea, where the arch was forty-six feet in height. The breakers dashed far into the cave, and flocks of sea-birds circled round its mouth. The sound of a gun was like a deafening peal of thunder, crashing from arch to arch till it rolled out of the cavern.

On the top of the hill a splendid hotel is erected for visitors to the Causeway; after passing this we descended to the base of the cliffs, which are here upward of four hundred feet high, and soon began to find in the columnar formation of the rocks indications of our approach. The guide pointed out some columns which appeared to have been melted and run together, from which Sir Humphrey Davy attributed the formation of the Causeway to the action of fire. Near this is the Giant's Well, a spring of the purest water, the bottom formed by three perfect hexagons and the sides of regular columns. One of us observing that no giant had ever drunk from it, the old man answered. "Perhaps not, but it was made by a giant—God Almighty!"

From the well the Causeway commences—a mass

of columns from triangular to octagonal, lying in compact forms and extending into the sea. I was somewhat disappointed at first, having supposed the Causeway to be of great height, but I found the Giant's Loom, which is the highest part of it, to be but about fifty feet from the water. The singular appearance of the columns and the many strange forms which they assume render it, nevertheless, an object of the greatest interest. Walking out on the rocks, we came to the Ladies' Chair, the seat, back sides and foot-stool being all regularly formed by the broken columns. The guide said that any lady who would take three drinks from the Giant's Well, then sit in this chair and think of any gentleman for whom she had a preference, would be married before a twelvemonth. I asked him if it would answer as well for gentlemen, for by a wonderful coincidence we had each drank three times at the well. He said it would, and thought he was confirming his statement.

A cluster of columns about half-way up the cliff is called the Giant's Organ from its very striking resemblance to that instrument, and a single rock worn by the waves into the shape of a rude seat is his chair. A mile or two farther along the coast two cliffs project from the range, leaving a vast semicircular space between, which from its resemblance to the old Roman theaters was appropriated for that purpose by the giant. Halfway down the crags are two or three pinnacles of rock called the Chimneys, and the stumps of several others can be seen, which, it is said, were shot off by a vessel belonging to the Spanish Armada in mistake for the towers

IRELAND

of Dunluce Castle. The vessel was afterward wrecked in the bay below, which has ever since been called Spanish Bay, and in calm weather the wreck may be still seen. Many of the columns of the Causeway have been carried off and sold as pillars for mantels, and tho a notice is put up threatening any one with the rigor of the law, depredations are occasionally made.

Returning, we left the road at Dunluce and took a path which led along the summit of the cliffs. The twilight was gathering and the wind blew with perfect fury, which, combined with the black and stormy sky, gave the coast an air of extreme wildness. All at once, as we followed the winding path, the crags, appeared to open before us, disclosing a yawning chasm down which a large stream falling in an unbroken sheet was lost in the gloom below. Witnessed in a calm day, there may perhaps be nothing striking about it, but coming upon us at once through the gloom of twilight, with the sea thundering below and a scowling sky above, it was absolutely startling. The path at last wound with many a steep and slippery bend down the almost perpendicular crags to the shore at the foot of a giant isolated rock having a natural arch through it, eighty feet in height. We followed the narrow strip of beach, having the bare crags on one side and a line of foaming breakers on the other. It soon grew dark; a furious storm came up and swept like a hurricane along the shore. I then understood what Horne means by "the lengthening javelins of the blast," for every drop seemed to strike with the force of an arrow, and our clothes were soon pierced in every part.

Then we went up among the sand-hills and lost each other in the darkness, when, after stumbling about among the gullies for half an hour shouting for my companions, I found the road and heard my call answered; but it happened to be two Irishmen, who came up and said, "And is it another gintleman ye're callin' for? We heard some one cryin,' and didn't know but somebody might be kilt."

Finally, about eleven o'clock, we all arrived at the inn dripping with rain, and before a warm fire concluded the adventures of our day in Ireland.

CORK*

BY WILLIAM MAKEPEACE THACKERAY.

One sees in this country many a grand and tall iron gate leading into a very shabby field covered with thistles; and the simile of the gate will in some degree apply to this famous city of Cork—which is certainly not a city of palaces, but of which the outlets are magnificent. That toward Killarney leads by the Lee, the old Avenue of Mardyke, and the rich green pastures stretching down to the river; and as you pass by the portico of the country jail, as fine and as glancing as a palace, you see the wooded heights on the other side of the fair stream, crowded with a thousand pretty villas and terraces, presenting every image of comfort and prosperity.

Along the quays up to St. Patrick's Bridge

*From "The Irish Sketch Book."

there is a certain bustle. Some forty ships may be lying at anchor along the walls of the quay; and its pavements are covered with goods of various merchandise; here a cargo of hides; yonder a company of soldiers, their kits, and their dollies, who are taking leave of the redcoats at the steamer's side. Then you shall see a fine, squeaking, shrieking drove of pigs embarking by the same conveyance, and insinuated into the steamer by all sorts of coaxing, threatening, and wheedling. Seamen are singing and yeehoing on board; grimy colliers smoking at the liquor-shops along the quay; and as for the bridge—there is a crowd of idlers on that, you may be sure, sprawling over the balustrade for ever and ever, with long ragged coats, steeple-hats, and stumpy doodeens.

At the other extremity of the town, if it be assize time, you will see some five hundred persons squatting in the Court-house, or buzzing and talking within; the rest of the respectable quarter of the city is pretty free from anything like bustle. There is no more life in Patrick Street than in Russell Square of a sunshiny day; and as for the Mall, it is as lonely as the chief street of a German Residenz. . . . That the city contains much wealth is evidenced by the number of handsome villas round about it, where the rich merchants dwell; but the warehouses of the wealthy provision-merchants make no show to the stranger walking the streets; and of the retail shops, if some are spacious and handsome, most look as if too big for the business carried on within. The want of ready money was quite curious. In three of the principal shops I purchased articles, and tendered a pound in exchange—not one of them had silver enough; and as for a five-pound note, which I presented at one of the topping booksellers, his boy went round to various places in vain, and finally set forth to the bank, where change was got. In another small shop I offered half-a-crown to pay for a sixpenny article—it was all the same.

Half a dozen of the public buildings I saw were spacious and shabby beyond all cockney belief. Adjoining the Imperial Hotel is a great, large, handsome, desolate reading-room, which was founded by a body of Cork merchants and tradesmen, and is the very picture of decay. Not Palmyra—not the Russell Institution in Great Coram Street—present more melancholy appearances of faded greatness. Opposite this is another institution, called the Cork Library, where there are plenty of books and plenty of kindness to the stranger; but the shabbiness and faded splendor of the place are quite painful. . . . . I have said something in praise of the manners of the Cork ladies; in regard of the gentlemen, a stranger must remark the extraordinary degree of literary taste and talent among them, and the wit and vivacity of their conversation. The love for literature seems to an Englishman doubly curious. What, generally speaking, do a company of grave gentlemen and ladies in Baker Street know about it? Who ever reads books in the City, or how often does one hear them talked about at a Club? The Cork citizens are the most book-loving men I ever met. The town has sent to England a number of literary men, of reputation too, and is not a little proud of their fame. Everybody seemed to know what Maginn was doing, and that Father Prout had a third volume ready, and what was Mr. Croker's last article in the Quarterly. The clerks and shopmen seemed as much "au fait" as their employers, and many is the conversation I heard about the merits of this writer or that—Dickens, Ainsworth, Lover, Lever.

I think, in walking the streets, and looking at the ragged urchins crowding there, every Englishman must remark that the superiority of intelligence is here, and not with us. I never saw such a collection of bright-eyed, wild, clever, eager faces. Mr. Maclise has carried away a number of them in his memory; and the lovers of his admirable pictures will find more than one Munster countenance under a helmet in company of Macbeth, or in a slashed doublet alongside of Prince Hamlet, or in the very midst of Spain in company with Signor Gil Blas. Gil Blas himself came from Cork, and not from Oviedo.

I listened to two boys almost in rags: they were lolling over the quay balustrade, and talking about one of the Ptolemys! and talking very well too. One of them had been reading in Rollin, and was detailing his information with a great deal of eloquence and fire. Another day, walking in the Mardyke, I followed three boys, not half so well drest as London errand-boys: one was telling the other about Captain Ross's voyages, and spoke with as much brightness and intelligence as the best-read gentleman's son in England could do. He was as much of a gentleman, too, the ragged young student; his manner as good, tho perhaps more eager and emphatic; his language was extremely rich, too, and eloquent. Does the reader remember his school-days, when half a dozen lads in the bedrooms took it by turns to tell stories? How poor the language generally was, and how exceedingly poor the imagination! Both of those ragged Irish lads had the making of gentlemen, scholars, orators, in them.

I have just been strolling up a pretty little height called Grattan's Hill, that overlooks the town and the river, and where the artist that comes Corkward may find many subjects for his pencil. There is a kind of pleasure-ground at the top of this eminence—a broad walk that draggles up to a ruined wall, with a ruined niche in it, and a battered stone bench. On the side that shelves down to the water are some beeches, and opposite them a row of houses from which you see one of the prettiest prospects possible—the shining river with the craft along the quays, and the busy city in the distance, the active little steamers puffing away toward Cove, the farther bank crowned with rich woods, and pleasant-looking country-houses—perhaps they are tumbling, rickety, and ruinous, as those houses close by us, but you can't see the ruin from here.

What a strange air of forlorn gaiety there is about the place!—the sky itself seems as if it did not know whether to laugh or cry, so full is it of clouds and sunshine. Little fat, ragged, smiling children are clambering about the rocks, and sitting on mossy doorsteps, tending other children yet smaller, fatter, and more dirty. "Stop till I get you a posy" (pronounced pawawawsee), cries one urchin to another. "Tell me who is it ye love, Jooly," exclaims another, cuddling a red-faced infant with a very dirty nose. More of the same race are perched about the summer-house, and two wenches with large purple feet are flapping some carpets in the air. It is a wonder the carpets will bear this kind of treatment at all, and do not be off at once to mingle with the elements; I never saw things that hung to life by such a frail thread.

This dismal pleasant place is a suburb of the second city in Ireland, and one of the most beautiful spots about the town. What a prim, bustling, active, green-railinged, tea-gardened, gravel-walked place would it have been in the five-hundredth town in England!—but you see the people can be quite as happy in the rags and without the paint, and I hear a great deal more heartiness and affection from these children than from their fat little brethren across the Channel.

BLARNEY CASTLE*

BY MR. AND MRS. S. C. HALL

Few places in Ireland are more familiar to English ears than Blarney; the notoriety is attributable, first, to the marvellous qualities of its famous "stone," and next, to the extensive popularity of the song,—

"The groves of Blarney, they are so charming."

When or how the stone obtained its singular reputation, it is difficult to determine; the exact position among the ruins of the castle is also a matter of doubt; the peasant-guides humor the

*From "Ireland: Its Scenery, Character, Etc."

visitor according to his capacity for climbing, and direct, either to the summit or the base, the attention of him who desires to "greet it with a holy kiss." He who has been dipt in the Shannon is presumed to have obtained, in abundance, the gift of that "civil courage" which makes an Irishman at ease and unconstrained in all places and under all circumstances; and he who has kissed the Blarney stone is assumed to be endowed with a fluent and persuasive tongue, altho it may be associated with insincerity; the term "Blarney" being generally used to characterize words that are meant neither to be "honest nor true."

It is conjectured that the comparatively modern application of the term "Blarney" first had existence when the possessor, Lord Clancarty, was a prisoner to Sir George Carew, by whom he was subjected to several examinations touching his loyalty, which he was required to prove by surrendering his strong castle to the soldiers of the Queen; this act he always endeavored to evade by some plausible excuse, but as invariably professing his willingness to do so. The particulars are fully detailed in the "Pacata Hibernia."

It is certain that to no particular stone of the ancient structure is the marvelous quality exclusively attributed; but in order to make it as difficult as possible to attain the enviable gift, it had long been the custom to point out a stone, a few feet below the battlements, which the very daring only would run the hazard of touching with their lips. The attempt to do so was, indeed, so dangerous, that a few years ago Mr. Jeffreys had it removed from the wall and placed on the highest point of the building; where the visitor

IRELAND

may now greet it with little risk. It is about two feet square, and contains the date 1703, with a portion of the arms of the Jeffreys family, but the date, at once, negatives its claim to be considered the true marvel of Blarney. A few days before our visit a madman made his way to the top of the castle, and after dancing round it for some hours, his escape from death being almost miraculous, he flung this stone from the tower; it was broken in the fall, and now, as the guide stated to us, the "three halves" must receive three distinct kisses to be in any degree effective.

The stronghold of Blarney was erected about the middle of the fifteenth century by Cormac Mac Carthy, surnamed "Laider," or the Strong; whose ancestors had been chieftains in Munster from a period long antecedent to the English invasion, and whose descendants, as Lords of Muskerry and Clancarty, retained no inconsiderable portion of their power and estates until the year 1689, when their immense possessions were confiscated, and the last earl became an exile, like the monarch whose cause he had supported. The castle, village, mills, fairs, and customs of Blarney, with the land and park thereunto belonging, containing 1400 acres, were "set up by cant" in the year 1702, purchased by Sir Richard Pyne, Lord Chief Justice, for £3000, and by him disposed of, the following year, to General Sir James Jeffreys, in whose family the property continues. Altho the walls of this castle are still strong, many of the outworks have long since been leveled; the plow has passed over their foundations, and "the stones of which they were built have been used in repairing the turnpike-roads."

MUCROSS ABBEY*

BY MR. AND MRS. S. C. HALL

The abbey of Mucross adjoins the pretty village of Cloghreen, [in Kerry] and is in the demesne of Henry Arthur Herbert, Esq., which includes the whole of the peninsula. The site was chosen with the usual judgment and taste of "the monks of old," who invariably selected the pleasantest of all pleasant places. The original name was Irelough—and it appears that long prior to the erection of this, now ruined structure, a church existed in the same spot, which was consumed by fire in 1191. The abbey was built for Franciscan monks, according to Archdall, in 1440; but the annals of the Four Masters give its date a century earlier: both, however, ascribe its foundation to one of the Mac Carthys, princes of Desmond. It was several times repaired, and once subsequently to the Reformation, as we learn from the inscription on a stone let into the north wall of the choir.

The building consists of two principal parts— the convent and the church. The church is about one hundred feet in length and twenty-four in breadth; the steeple, which stands between the nave and the chancel, rests on four high and slender pointed arches. The principal entrance is by a handsome pointed door-way, luxuriantly overgrown with ivy, through which is seen the great eastern window. The intermediate space, as indeed every part of the ruined edifice, is filled with

*From "Ireland: Its Scenery, Character, Etc."

tombs, the greater number distinguished only by a slight elevation from the mold around them; but some containing inscriptions to direct the stranger where especial honor should be paid. A large modern tomb, in the center of the choir, covers the vault, in which in ancient times were interred the Mac Carthys Mor, and more recently the O'Donoghue Mor of the Glens, whose descendants were buried here so late as the year 1833.

Close to this tomb, but on a level with the earth, is the slab which formerly covered the vault. It is without inscription, but bears the arms of the Earl of Clancarty. The convent as well as the church is in very tolerable preservation; and Mr. Herbert has taken especial care, as far as he can, to balk the consumer, time, of the remnants of his glorious feast. He has repaired the foundations in some parts and the parapets in others, and so judiciously that the eye is never annoyed by the intrusion of the new among the old; the ivy furnishing him with a ready means for hiding the unhallowed brick and mortar from the sight. In his "caretaker," too, he has a valuable auxiliary; and a watch is set, first to discover tokens of decay, then to prevent their spread, and then to twist and twine the young shoots of the aged trees over and around them.

The dormitories, the kitchen, the refectory, the cellars, the infirmary, and other chambers, are still in a state of comparative preservation; the upper rooms are unroofed; and the coarse grass grows abundantly among them. The great fireplace of the refectory is curious and interesting —affording evidence that the good monks were not forgetful of the duty they owed themselves, or of the bond they had entered into, to act upon the advice of St. Paul, and be "given to hospitality." This recess is pointed out as the bed of John Drake—a pilgrim who, about a century ago, took up his abode in the Abbey, and continued its inmate during a period of several years. As will be supposed, his singular choice of residence has given rise to abundant stories, and the mention of his name to any of the guides or boatmen will at once produce a volume of the marvelous.

The cloister, which consists of twenty-two arches, ten of them semicircular and twelve pointed, is the best preserved portion of the abbey. In the center grows a magnificent yew-tree, which covers, as a roof, the whole area; its circumference is thirteen feet, and its height in proportion. It is more than probable that the tree is coeval with the abbey; that it was planted by the hands of the monks who built the sacred edifice centuries ago. The yew, it is known, lives to a prodigious age; and in England, there are many of a date considerably earlier than that which may be safely assigned to this.

FROM GLENGARIFF TO KILLARNEY*

BY WILLIAM MAKEPEACE THACKERAY

The journey from Glengariff to Kenmare is one of astonishing beauty; and I have seen Killarney since, and am sure that Glengariff loses

*From "The Irish Sketch Book."

IRELAND

nothing by comparison with this most famous of lakes. Rock, wood, and sea stretch around the traveler—a thousand delightful pictures; the landscape is at first wild without being fierce, immense woods and plantations enriching the valleys—beautiful streams to be seen everywhere.

Here again I was surprised at the great population along the road; for one saw but few cabins, and there is no village between Glengariff and Kenmare. But men and women were on banks and in fields; children, as usual, came trooping up to the car; and the jovial men of the yacht had great conversations with most of the persons whom we met on the road. A merrier set of fellows it were hard to meet.

After much mountain-work of ascending and descending (in which latter operation, and by the side of precipices that make passing cockneys rather squeamish, the carman drove like mad to the hooping and screeching of the red rovers), we at length came to Kenmare, of which all that I know is that it lies prettily in a bay or arm of the sea; that it is approached by a little hanging-bridge, which seems to be a wonder in these parts; that it is a miserable little place when you enter it; and that, finally, a splendid luncheon of all sorts of meat and excellent cold salmon may sometimes be had for a shilling at the hotel of the place. . . . . For almost half the way from Kenmare, this wild, beautiful road commands views of the famous lake and vast blue mountains about Killarney. Turk, Tomies, and Mangerton were clothed in purple like kings in mourning; great heavy clouds were gathered round their noble features bare. The lake lay for some time underneath us, dark and blue, with dark misty islands in the midst. On the right-hand side of the road would be a precipice covered with a thousand trees, or a green rocky flat, with a reedy mere in the midst, and other mountains rising as far as we could see. . . . . And so it was that we rode by dark old Mangerton, then presently past Mucross, and then through two miles of avenues of lime-trees, by numerous lodges and gentlemen's seats, across an old bridge, where you see the mountains again and the lake, until, by Lord Kenmare's house, a hideous row of houses informed us that we were in Killarney.

We rattled up to the Kenmare Arms; and so ended, not without a sigh on my part, one of the merriest six-hour rides that five yachtsmen, one cockney, five women and a child, the carman, and a countryman with an alpeen, ever took in their lives. The town of Killarney was in a violent state of excitement with a series of horse-races, hurdle-races, boat-races, and stag-hunts by land and water, which were taking place, and attracted a vast crowd from all parts of the kingdom. All the inns were full, and lodgings cost five shillings a day, nay, more in some places; for tho my landlady, Mrs. Macgillicuddy, charges but that sum, a leisurely old gentleman whom I never saw in my life before made my acquaintance by stopping me in the street yesterday, and said he paid a pound a day for his two bedrooms. . . . . Mrs. Macgillicuddy's house is at the corner of the two principal streets in Killarney town, and the drawing-room windows command each a street. A sort of market is held there, and the place is swarming with blue cloaks and groups of

IRELAND

men talking; here and there is a stall with coarse linens, crockery, a cheese; and crowds of egg- and milk-women are squatted on the pavement, with their ragged customers or gossips. Carts, cars, jingles, barouches, horses, and vehicles of all descriptions rattle presently through the streets; for the town is crowded with company for the races and other sports, and all the world is bent to see the stag-hunt on the lake.

The morning had been bright enough, but for fear of accidents we took our macintoshes, and at about a mile from the town found it necessary to assume those garments and wear them for the greater part of the day. Passing by the Victoria, with its beautiful walks, park, and lodge, we came to a little creek where the boats were moored; and there was the wonderful lake before us, with its mountains, and islands, and trees. Unluckily, however, the mountains happened to be invisible; the islands looked like gray masses in the fog, and all that we could see for some time was the gray silhouette of the boat ahead of us, in which a passenger was engaged in a witty conversation with some boat still farther in the mist.

Drumming and trumpeting was heard at a little distance, and presently we found ourselves in the midst of a fleet of boats upon the rocky shores of the beautiful little Innisfallen. Here we landed for a while, and the weather clearing up, allowed us to see this charming spot. Rocks, shrubs, and little abrupt rises and falls of ground, covered with the brightest emerald grass; a beautiful little ruin of a Saxon chapel, lying gentle, delicate, and plaintive on the shore;

some noble trees round about it, and beyond, presently, the tower of Ross Castle, island after island appearing in the clearing sunshine, and the huge hills throwing their misty veils off, and wearing their noble robes of purple. The boats' crews were grouped about the place, and one large barge especially had landed some sixty people, being the Temperance band, with its drums, trumpets, and wives. They were marshaled by a grave old gentleman with a white waistcoat and queue, a silver medal decorating one side of his coat, and a brass heart reposing on the other flap. The horns performed some Irish airs prettily; and, at length, at the instigation of a fellow who went swaggering about with a pair of whirling drumsticks, all formed together, and played "Garryowen"—the active drum of course most dreadfully out of time.

Having strolled about the island for a quarter of an hour, it became time to take to the boats again, and we were rowed over to the wood opposite Sullivan's cascade, where the hounds had been laid in in the morning, and the stag was expected to take water. Fifty or sixty men are employed on the mountain to drive the stag lakeward, should he be inclined to break away; and the sport generally ends by the stag, a wild one, making for the water with the pack swimming afterward; and here he is taken and disposed of, how I know not. It is rather a parade than a stag-hunt; but, with all the boats around and the noble view, must be a fine thing to see.

Some scores more boats were there, darting up and down in the pretty, busy waters. Here came a Cambridge boat; and where, indeed, will not the gentlemen of that renowned University be found? Yonder were the dandy dragoons, stiff, silent, slim, faultlessly appointed, solemnly puffing cigars. Every now and then a hound would be heard in the wood, whereon numbers of voices, right and left, would begin to yell in chorus—Hurroo! Hoop! Yow—yow—yow! in accents the most shrill or the most melancholious. Meanwhile the sun had had enough of the sport, the mountains put on their veils again, the islands retreated into the mist, the word went through the fleet to spread all umbrellas, and ladies took shares of mackintoshes and disappeared under the flaps of silk cloaks.

The wood comes down to the very edge of the water, and many of the crews thought fit to land and seek this green shelter. To behold these moist dandies the natives of the country came eagerly. Strange, savage faces might be seen peering from out of the trees; long-haired, bare-legged girls came down the hill, some with green apples and very sickly-looking plums; some with whisky and goat's milk; a ragged boy had a pair of stag's-horns to sell: the place swarmed with people. We went up the hill to see the noble cascade, and when you say that it comes rushing down over rocks and through tangled woods, alas!, one has said all the dictionary can help you to, and not enough to distinguish this particular cataract from any other. This seen and admired, we came back to the harbor where the boats lay, and from which spot the reader might have seen the following view of the lake—that is, you would see the lake, if the mist would only clear away.

But this for hours it did not seem inclined to do. We rowed up and down industriously for a period of time which seemed to me atrociously long. The bugles of the Erin had long since sounded "Home, sweet home!" and the greater part of the fleet had dispersed. As for the stag-hunt, all I saw of it was four dogs that appeared on the shore at different intervals, and a huntsman in a scarlet coat, who similarly came and went: once or twice we were gratified by hearing the hounds; but at last it was agreed that there was no chance for the day, and we rowed off to Kenmare Cottage—where, on the lovely lawn, or in a cottage adjoining, the gentry picnic, and where, with a handkerchief full of potatoes, we made as pleasant a meal as ever I recollect.

What is to be said about Turk Lake? When there, we agreed that it was more beautiful than the larger lake, of which it is not one-fourth the size; then, when we came back, we said, "No, the large lake is the most beautiful." And so, at every point we stopped at, we determined that that particular spot was the prettiest in the whole lake. The fact is, and I don't care to own it, they are too handsome. As for a man coming from his desk in London or Dublin and seeing "the whole lakes in a day," he is an ass for his pains; a child doing sums in addition might as well read the whole multiplication table, and fancy he had it by heart. We should look at these wonderful things leisurely and thoughtfully; and even then, blessed is he who understands them.

ANNE HATHAWAY'S COTTAGE, NEAR STRATFORD

ROOM IN STRATFORD IN WHICH SHAKESPEARE WAS BORN

STRATFORD-ON-AVON
(See Vol. I for article on Stratford)

INTERIOR OF TRINITY CHURCH, STRATFORD
Within the Chancel is Shakespeare's Grave

LIST OF ILLUSTRATIONS

FOLLOWING PAGE 96

    STIRLING CASTLE
    RUINS OF HOLYROOD ABBEY, EDINBURGH
    MELROSE ABBEY
    GLASTONBURY ABBEY
    CRAIGMILLAR CASTLE, SCOTLAND
    DUNBARTON ROCK AND CASTLE
    LIMERICK CASTLE
    ST. PATRICK'S CATHEDRAL, DUBLIN
    THE GIANT'S CAUSEWAY
    BLARNEY CASTLE
    MUCROSS ABBEY
    THE LAKES OF KILLARNEY
    SACKVILLE STREET, DUBLIN
    THE GAP OF DUNLOE

LIST OF ILLUSTRATIONS

VOLUME II

FRONTISPIECE

    Princess Street and Scott's Monument, Edinburgh

PRECEDING PAGE 1

    Stratford-on-Avon
    Interior of Trinity Church, Stratford
    Anne Hathaway's Cottage, Near Stratford
    Room in Stratford in Which Shakespeare Was Born
    Newstead Abbey, Byron's Ancestral Home
    Stoke Pogis, the Scene of Gray's "Elegy"
    Oxford
    Eddystone Lighthouse
    St. Martin's Church, Canterbury
    Edinburgh Castle and National Gallery
    Old Greyfriar's Church, Edinburgh
    Holyrood Palace, Edinburgh

CONTENTS

VII—IRELAND

	PAGE
A Summer Day in Dublin—By William Makepeace Thackeray	149
Dublin Castle—By Mr. and Mrs. S. C. Hall	157
St. Patrick's Cathedral—By Mr. and Mrs. S. C. Hall	160
Limerick—By Mr. and Mrs. S. C Hall	162
From Belfast to Dublin—By William Cullen Bryant	167
The Giant's Causeway—By Bayard Taylor	172
Cork—By William Makepeace Thackeray	176
Blarney Castle—By Mr. and Mrs. S. C. Hall	181
Mucross Abbey—By Mr. and Mrs. S. C. Hall	184
From Glengariff to Killarney—By William Makepeace Thackeray	186

CONTENTS

VI—SCOTLAND

	PAGE
EDINBURGH—By Robert Louis Stevenson	67
HOLYROOD—By David Masson	75
LINLITHGOW—By Sir Walter Scott	78
STIRLING—By Nathaniel Hawthorne	83
ABBOTSFORD—By William Howitt	86
DRYBURGH ABBEY—By William Howitt	92
MELROSE ABBEY—By William Howitt	98
CARLYLE'S BIRTHPLACE AND EARLY HOMES—By John Burroughs	104
BURNS'S LAND—By Nathaniel Hawthorne	108
HIGHLAND MARY'S HOME AND GRAVE—By Theodore F. Wolfe	122
THROUGH THE CALEDONIA CANAL TO INVERNESS—By H. A. Taine	128
THE SCOTCH HIGHLANDS—By H. A. Taine	132
BEN LOMOND AND THE HIGHLAND LAKES—By Bayard Taylor	134
TO THE HEBRIDES—By James Boswell	140
STAFFA AND IONA—By William Howitt	143

CONTENTS OF VOLUME II

Great Britain and Ireland—Part Two

IV—ENGLISH LITERARY SHRINES—
(*Continued*)

	PAGE
STOKE POGIS—By Charles T. Congdon	1
HAWORTH—By Theodore F. Wolfe	7
GAD'S HILL—By Theodore F. Wolfe	14
RYDAL MOUNT—By William Howitt	20
TWICKENHAM—By William Howitt	22

V—OTHER ENGLISH SCENES

STONEHENGE—By Ralph Waldo Emerson	27
MAGNA CHARTA ISLAND—By Mrs. S. C. Hall	30
THE HOME OF THE PILGRIM FATHERS—By James M. Hoppin	33
OXFORD—By Goldwin Smith	37
CAMBRIDGE—By James M. Hoppin	44
CHESTER—By Nathaniel Hawthorne	51
EDDYSTONE LIGHTHOUSE—By Frederick A. Talbot	54
THE CAPITAL OF THE BRITISH, SAXON AND NORMAN KINGS—By William Howitt	61

Copyright, 1914, by
FUNK & WAGNALLS COMPANY
[*Printed in the United States of America*]

SEEING EUROPE
WITH FAMOUS AUTHORS

SELECTED AND EDITED

WITH

INTRODUCTIONS, ETC.

BY

FRANCIS W. HALSEY

Editor of "Great Epochs in American History"
Associate Editor of "The World's Famous Orations"
and of "The Best of the World's Classics," etc.

IN TEN

VOLUMES

ILLUSTRATED

Vol. II

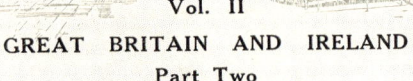

GREAT BRITAIN AND IRELAND
Part Two

FUNK & WAGNALLS COMPANY

NEW YORK AND LONDON

PRINCES STREET AND SCOTT'S MONUMENT, EDINBURGH